Ssu-Ch'ing: The Socialist Education Movement of 1962-1966

A publication of the
Center for Chinese Studies
University of California,
Berkeley, California 94720

Cover Colophon by Shih-hsiang Chen.

Center for Chinese Studies • CHINA RESEARCH MONOGRAPHS
UNIVERSITY OF CALIFORNIA, BERKELEY

/ NUMBER TWO

Ssu-Ch'ing: The Socialist Education Movement of 1962-1966

RICHARD BAUM
and FREDERICK C. TEIWES

Although the Center for Chinese Studies is responsible for the selection and acceptance of monographs in this series, responsibility for the opinions expressed in them and for the accuracy of statements contained in them rests with their authors.

Foreword

Perhaps the least anticipated aspect of Mao Tse-tung's Great Proletarian Cultural Revolution was his attack on and virtual discrediting of the entire Communist Party apparatus throughout China. Clearly enough, the Party had failed him in significant ways—but in ways that were far from clear to the external observer of Chinese politics. It appears now that the crucial period 1962–66 was a turning point. Mao and the Party tried to overcome the undesirable consequences, from their point of view, of the post-Great Leap Forward crisis and the emergency measures taken to alleviate the crisis. However, differing estimates of these undesirable conditions and differing approaches to overcoming them tended to set Mao against the Party and thereby set the stage for the Cultural Revolution confrontation.

The key event of this period was the Socialist Education Movement. Richard Baum and Frederick C. Teiwes, in their monographic study of this most important political movement in China immediately prior to the Cultural Revolution, have helped to elucidate both the Socialist Education Movement itself and the subsequent upheaval. This study is noteworthy both for its careful analysis of the political events of the period and for its making available new and important documentation that may assist research on other aspects of the Socialist Education Movement period.

Richard Baum is a Ph.D. candidate in political science at the University of California, Berkeley, and is currently completing his dissertation research in Hong Kong. He was a fellow of the Center for Chinese Studies from 1962 to 1966, and he has contributed articles to *Asian Survey, The China Quarterly, Far Eastern Economic Review,* and *Western Political Quarterly.* Mr. Baum has accepted an appointment as Assistant Professor of Political Science, University of California, Los Angeles.

Frederick C. Teiwes is a Ph.D. candidate in the Department of Public Law and Government, Columbia University. Having carried out research in Hong Kong and Taiwan, he is completing a dissertation on "Rectification Campaigns and Purges in Communist China." Mr. Teiwes has contributed to *Asian Survey* and *The China Quarterly,* and he is the author of *Provincial Party Personnel in Mainland China, 1956–1966* (New York: East Asian Institute Occasional Papers, Columbia University, 1967).

John S. Service of the Center for Chinese Studies checked the translations included in this study and worked with the authors to insure the accuracy of the sources for their analysis of a difficult period.

CHALMERS JOHNSON, *Chairman*
Center for Chinese Studies

Berkeley, California
February, 1968

Contents

AUTHOR'S ACKNOWLEDGMENTS

The authors would like to acknowledge the invaluable assistance rendered by the scholars and administrative staff of the Universities Service Centre, Hong Kong, in the preparation, editing, and typing of the manuscript. A special debt of gratitude is owed to David Denny, Frederic Surls and Carolyn Baum for their editorial suggestions. In addition, we also wish to thank the Director and staff of the Institute of International Relations, Republic of China, for making available to us their collection of documentary materials on the Socialist Education Movement. Finally, we are indebted to the Foreign Area Fellowship Program, the Fulbright-Hayes Program, the Columbia University East Asian Institute, and the University of California Center for Chinese Studies for the financial and moral support that made this research possible. Needless to say, the authors assume sole responsibility for any of the views expressed or conclusions reached in this study.

ABBREVIATIONS

CB *Current Background*
CCP Chinese Communist Party
JMJP *Jen-min Jih-pao*
NCNA New China News Agency
NFJP *Nan-fang Jih-pao*
SCMM *Selections from China Mainland Magazines*
SCMP *Survey of China Mainland Press*

Introduction

The Socialist Education Movement of 1962–1966 has been, for the outside observer, one of the most poorly documented and least understood of political developments on the Chinese mainland during the years since the Great Leap. If only for scope, intensity, and duration, the movement merits the serious attention of the student of Communist China. The passage of time, moreover, has underlined its importance. Great historical significance, for instance, has now been attributed to it by proponents of the Great Proletarian Cultural Revolution. In the speeches of Party leaders, in the editorials of official media, and in Red Guard publications, it has been acclaimed as the direct antecedent of the Cultural Revolution. And some of the most serious charges against "the handful of people in positions of authority within the Party who take the capitalist road" have their basis in the leadership and implementation of this Movement.[1]

Scholars have, of course, realized that the Socialist Education Movement was important. But because basic and authoritative documentary materials had not reached Western scholars, the details of its history, nature, and significance have remained enigmatic and obscure. This situation has now changed. There has recently become available, through Chinese Nationalist sources, a lengthy and detailed set of Chinese Communist Party Central Committee directives which bear directly on the aims and instrumentalities of the Movement. These include the full texts of four fundamental policy statements: the First Ten Points (ch'ien shih t'iao)[2] of May 1963; the Later Ten Points (hou shih t'iao)[3] of September 1963; the September 1964 revised draft of the Later Ten Points;[4] and the Twenty-three Articles (erh-shih-san t'iao)[5] of January 1965. Also available is a set of regulations, dated June 1964, concerning the organization of peasant associations.[6]

---

[1] For a more detailed examination of this latter question, see Baum and Teiwes, "Liu Shao-ch'i and the Cadre Question," *Asian Survey*, Vol. VIII, No. 4 (April, 1968).

[2] "Draft Resolution of the Central Committee of the Chinese Communist Party on Some Problems in Current Rural Work": see Appendix B for translation of text.

[3] "Some Concrete Policy Formulations of the Central Committee of the Chinese Communist Party in the Rural Socialist Education Movement (Draft)": see Appendix C for translation of text.

[4] "Some Concrete Policy Formulations of the Central Committee of the Chinese Communist Party in the Rural Socialist Education Movement (Revised Draft)": see Appendix E for translation of excerpts.

[5] "Some Problems Currently Arising in the Course of the Rural Socialist Education Movement": see Appendix F for translation of text.

A close analysis of these five documents, combined with an intensive survey of mainland press and radio materials originating during the period, now makes possible this attempt at an overall assessment of the causes, concomitants, and consequences of the Socialist Education Movement.

The focus of this study will be on the rural components of the Socialist Education Movement. This concentration on the rural may risk eliminating a part of the picture. There have, for instance, been a number of references in the Chinese media to socialist education work in many of the urban areas of China during the 1962–1966 period. From what is known, however, the general contours of this urban movement seemed to parallel closely the rural prototypes. Moreover, the CCP directives of which we have knowledge—and which are used in this study—pertain almost exclusively to the rural areas. In the interests of economy and integrity, we have therefore concentrated on the rural aspects of the Movement as being those which offered the greatest promise in terms of useful research.

Throughout this study the term "cadre" *(kan-pu)* is used freely and frequently. This generic term refers to all personnel who perform official functions in any organization in China—from the lowest clerk in a government agency to the Chairman of the CCP Central Committee. Cadres are not necessarily Party members, and Party members are not necessarily cadres. The term "basic-level cadres" *(chi-ts'eng kan-pu)* is used in this study to refer to officials at the lowest levels of their respective organizations. In rural areas the term is applied to all cadres at the levels of production brigade and production team regardless of rank or status. The term "leading cadre" *(ling-tao kan-pu),* on the other hand, denotes top ranking executive and supervisory personnel at each level of the Party and state administrative structure. Thus the Party branch secretary of a production brigade would be considered a leading cadre, as would the head of the brigade's management committee, while ordinary branch members and brigade cadres would not be so designated. Both the leaders and ordinary brigade officials, however, would be basic-level cadres.

Of the primary CCP documents and directives used in the preparation of this study, the Twenty-three Articles and the peasant association regulations were translated by the authors from the Chinese originals. The remaining documents were translated by the government of the Republic of China. In all cases the English translations have been checked against the Chinese originals. In addition, the excerpts from the Lienchiang documents which appear in the Appendix have also been closely checked against the Chinese text.

---

[6] "Organizational Rules of Poor and Lower-middle Peasants Associations": see Appendix D for translation of text.

I
Origins and Experimentation

Foreshadowings of the Socialist Education Movement can be seen in the reports of the Central Committee's Tenth Plenum, which took place in September 1962. The official communique of the Plenum presented a cautiously optimistic summary of current internal economic conditions. It then turned, however, to a discussion of shortcomings requiring attention.

> It should be pointed out that some of our work is not well done. For instance, because of the incompetence of the leading cadres, some production teams, some factories and some business establishments have produced less or become unwelcome to the masses. We should endeavor to change this state of affairs and improve the work of those units without delay.[1]

The guide line for an approach to the solution of these problems was a reaffirmation of the doctrine of class struggle.

> . . . . [T]hroughout the historical period of transition from capitalism to communism . . . . there is class struggle . . . . [T]here still exist in society bourgeois influence, the force of habit of old society and the spontaneous tendency toward capitalism among part of the small producers. Therefore, among the people, a small number of persons, making up only a tiny fraction of the total population, who have not yet undergone socialist remoulding, always attempt to depart from the socialist road and turn to the capitalist road whenever there is an opportunity. . . . [W]e must remain vigilant and resolutely oppose in good time various opportunistic ideological tendencies in the Party.[2]

What were the concrete realities behind all these vague warnings and exhortations about class struggle and shortcomings in Party work? A partial answer is provided by a unique set of documents which were captured by Chinese Nationalist commandos during a 1964 raid of Lienchiang hsien in Fukien. These so-called "Lienchiang documents" consisted of a series of internal Party communications—directions, reports, and statistical materials—covering a broad range of questions concerning the communes.[3] They are in effect a catalogue of develop-

---

[1] *Peking Review*, No. 39, 1962.
[2] *Ibid.*
[3] See *Fan-kung Yu-chi-tui T'u-chi Fu-chien Lien-chiang Lu-huo Fei-fang Wen-chien Hui-pien* (Collected Documents Captured During an Anti-communist Com-

ments in the communes of Lienchiang hsien during the six month period from October 1962 to March 1963. One document is of particular interest and a translation in full is reprinted as Appendix A.

This document is a report, dated February 9, 1963, to an enlarged hsien cadre meeting dealing with a recently launched socialist education movement. Much attention is devoted to "unhealthy tendencies" which had arisen among commune members and basic-level cadres during the "three lean years" of 1959–61 when a series of natural calamities, in combination with disastrous economic repercussions of the Great Leap, had necessitated a liberalization of the Party's agricultural policies.

A number of these "unhealthy tendencies" are described.

1) A "spontaneous inclination towards capitalism" of peasants, who preferred to "go it alone" and to rely for income on their private plots and individual sideline occupations rather than on collective undertakings.
2) A general relaxation of social and political controls, which permitted the rise of unorthodox practices such as abandoning farming to go into business, the squandering of funds, and speculation and gambling.
3) A revival of feudal practices such as religious festivals, money marriages, and spiritualist frauds and witchcraft.
4) A decline in morale of the cadres, many of whom complained that the rewards were incommensurate with the burdens and tensions of office and wished to resign.[4]
5) Actual corruption among cadres involving the misappropriation of public funds.

The situation in the Chinese countryside in the winter of 1962–1963, as reflected in the Lienchiang documents, was rather gloomy. Nevertheless, the prospects for reversing these potentially dangerous trends were held to be good. The instrument for this reversal was to be the Socialist Education Movement.

By the end of 1962—three months after the conclusion of the Tenth Plenum—the Socialist Education Movement was underway on a limited experimental basis in certain rural areas, including Lienchiang hsien. Where the movement had been launched, great progress was claimed to have already been made in improving the morale, work habits, and political consciousness of both cadres and masses.[5] It was still conceded,

---

mando Raid on Lienchiang hsien, Fukien). Taipei, Ministry of National Defense (Bureau of Intelligence), March, 1964 (microfilm, Center for Chinese Studies Library, University of California, Berkeley).

[4] *Ibid.* According to statistics presented in this document, such an attitude had been held by 172 cadres at the production brigade level and 1,016 cadres at the production team level in Lienchiang hsien alone—roughly 8 percent of the total number of basic-level cadres in the hsien. See Appendix A.

[5] There is ample indication that Lienchiang hsien was not unique in having been selected as a test site for launching the Socialist Education Movement in the fall

however, that "the level of our cadres, including our comrades at the hsien level, is not very high at present. We still do not sufficiently understand the experiences of struggle."[6]

The main problem appeared to be lack of effective leadership at the basic levels. To remedy this, in January 1963 leading cadres in the communes were instructed to take "appropriate steps," during their annual work of "readjusting the communes" *(cheng she)*, to raise the ideological, political, and managerial levels of basic-level cadres.[7] While the reasons for the weakness of leadership at the basic levels were held to be "numerous and complex," the single most common cause of difficulty was asserted to be the "impurity of basic-level cadres' work styles" *(tso-feng pu ch'un)*.[8]

The problem of leadership in the communes was linked to the question of class line in the countryside. The instruction was laid down: "When selecting and promoting cadres, comrades with backgrounds as poor and lower-middle peasants *(p'in hsia-chung nung)* should be given priority. This is because their class status and economic status enables them not to be too stubborn about preserving the system of small-scale private ownership of the means of production, and it enables them to accept socialism more readily." On the other hand, however, people of middle peasant *(chung nung)* and upper-middle peasant *(shang-chung nung)* origins were not to be automatically excluded from consideration for appointment or promotion as cadres, since "some of them have proved themselves . . . . to have a higher level of socialist consciousness."[9]

Toward those veteran cadres who had committed mistakes in carrying out their work, it was stated:

> Aside from those extremely few elements who persist in taking the capitalist road, ... and who ought to be given necessary punishment or necessary removal from their posts, with respect to the absolute majority of cadres who have shortcomings, it is a question of education; it is a question of using the method of criticism and self-criticism to reform their work styles.[10]

Accordingly, a policy of being "severe in ideological criticism and lenient in organizational treatment" was prescribed for solving ideological problems among the cadres. The objective was "to take warning from the

---

and winter of 1962–63; but the absence of any reliable data from other localities during this period precludes analysis of the scale and scope of the movement in this earliest stage.

6 *Ibid.*

7 *Jen-min Jih-pao* (People's Daily) [hereafter JMJP] Peking, January 1, 1963.

8 *JMJP*, January 11, 1963. It was further stated that this had been precisely the meaning of the reference, some three months earlier in the Tenth Plenum communique, to the "incompetence of leading personnel."

9 *Ibid.*

10 *Ibid.*

past in order to be more careful in the future" and "to treat the illness in order to save the man."[11]

The existence of a potentially critical basic level leadership gap in late 1962 and early 1963 also led to a renewed emphasis by the Party center on the policy of *hsia fang* (literally: downward transfer). To "earnestly strengthen the work of Party organizations in the countryside," it was decided to "send a number of outstanding Party members, cadres, and personnel who are loyal to the revolutionary cause . . . . who are capable workers, and who are well versed in the mass-line work method, to work in the countryside over a long duration."[12] By the end of February 1963, some 30,000 cadres from provincial, special district, hsien, and commune offices in Kwangtung province alone were reported to have entered basic-level units in the countryside in order to "help production team cadres with the leadership work in doing a good job of harvesting spring production."[13] These outside personnel were grouped into "work teams" *(kung-tso tui)* under responsible cadres. Upon entering the production brigades and teams, they were expected to eat, live, work, and consult with the basic level cadres and commune members, and to set a personal example in improving production work. They were also expected to mobilize the production team members to "study, compare, and catch up with" advanced production units, and render assistance to those units which were economically backward.[14] This sending of responsible cadres from higher levels down to the basic levels was referred to as "penetrating a point" *(shen-ju tao i-ko tien).*[15]

By the end of March 1963, experiences gained in various areas during the previous few months were summarized and publicized in the mass media. It was at this point that the Socialist Education Movement began to take shape as a systematic campaign. The first major policy directive concerning the implementation of the Movement was promulgated in May in the form of a "Draft Resolution of the Central Committee on Some Problems in Current Rural Work." (During later stages of the Movement this document came to be known as the First Ten Points and, for convenience, this simple title will be used below. The translation of the full text appears as Appendix B.)

The document itself purports to be based on extensive reports of rural conditions submitted by leading Party organs in the countryside.[16] Many

---

[11] *Hung Ch'i,* No. 2, 1963.

[12] *JMJP,* January 25, 1963.

[13] *JMJP,* February 23, 1963.

[14] *JMJP,* February 18, 1963.

[15] *JMJP,* February 23, 1963.

[16] See Appendix B, last paragraph of opening section. Twenty such reports—from commune to special district level in five provinces—were explicitly cited. The contents of these reports were apparently quite similar to the Lienchiang documents (see Appendix A).

of the dominant themes relating to the Party's rural work which had appeared in the press and radio during the seven month period since the Tenth Plenum were given fuller elaboration. Clearly, it was intended to set forth the broad directions the Socialist Education Movement was expected to take. But it seems also obvious that the drafters were more concerned with presenting problems to be solved on the basis of further experimentation than they were with providing complete and concrete policy guidelines for implementing the Movement.[17] The broad rubric was "class struggle" *(chieh-chi tou-cheng)*. The targets were both the peasant masses and the basic-level cadres. The methods were propaganda and education, emphasizing the need to strengthen the collective economy and dramatizing the history of the revolutionary struggle. The aim was to combat "unhealthy" rural conditions such as had been described in the Lienchiang documents.

The First Ten Points gave a concrete indication of what the regime considered to be "unclean" cadre work styles damaging the effectiveness of basic-level leadership. It introduced the term "Four Cleans" *(ssu-ch'ing)* as referring to the need to "clean up" accounts, granaries, properties, and work points.[18] Cadre corruption in those matters was held to be the greatest single cause of peasant dissatisfaction with the basic-level leadership in the countryside. Such corruption was adjudged to be an internal (non-antagonistic) contradiction among the people, and was to be handled primarily through methods of persuasive education. Furthermore, it was anticipated that the resolution of this contradiction would not be difficult to achieve; and the Four Cleans campaign was expected to result in the further consolidation of cadres and masses:

> As the masses put it: "The cadres toil the year round for the commune members. Their mistakes may be forgiven as long as they repent." Thus the cadres "dump their burdens," the masses feel free and easy, and cadres and masses are united more closely.[19]

The First Ten Points also sought to translate into concrete policy the concept of relying on the poor and lower-middle peasants. It called for the establishment of poor and lower-middle peasant organizations at the commune, brigade and production team levels. In attempting to define the functions of these organizations, Party leaders confronted a dilemma

---

[17] Appendix B, especially the introductory section and Article X. The preoccupation of the document's drafters with solving problems through practical experimentation is indicated by the inclusion of Mao's epistemological essay "Where Do Man's Correct Ideas Come From?", and by the injunction to Party committees, from hsien to provincial levels, to give high priority to study and research of the problems raised during experimental practice.

[18] The term "Four Cleans" (or "Four Cleanups") reportedly originated during investigations in Paoting special district, Hopeh, when peasants demanded the cleanup of accounts, granaries, properties, and work-points: *Ibid.*, Article VIII.

[19] *Ibid.*, Article VIII.

which was not easily resolved. Poor and lower-middle peasant groups were given a broad writ to oversee the work of commune and brigade level management committees, and the right to participate in deliberations on all important matters. But they were also warned against interfering in routine, day-to-day administrative affairs.[20] As is often the case with supervisory bodies, the powers of the poor and lower-middle peasant organizations were left ill-defined. This was to be a source of potential conflict.

The Party's concern with realizing the principles of the mass line was reflected in the demand raised in the First Ten Points that cadres must participate in collective productive labor "in accordance with regularized systems." Three years was set as the target period for regularized participation in production by the whole group of rural Party branch secretaries. It was to be considered a victory if one-third of this group participated during the first year.[21] This labor participation was intended not only to bring the cadres into close contact with the actual conditions of production and with the problems encountered by the peasants in their daily lives, but also to prevent the cadres from becoming bureaucrats and overlords, thus avoiding a situation likely to lead to revisionism.[22]

In discussing the general work methods of the campaign, the First Ten Points stressed the need for leading cadres to undertake investigations and experiments at selected points at the basic levels. Only in this way could responsible leaders collect data that were not superficial or one-sided, detect problems as they arose, and sum up experiences which would guide correctly the future development of the movement. With methods of leadership thus firmly grasped, and with correct handling of cadre problems, the outlook for the Socialist Education Movement was held to be relatively optimistic. Despite the solemn declaration that class struggle in the Chinese countryside was sharp and would continue over a considerable historical period, the directive anticipated that the basic tasks of the movement could be accomplished within three years.[23]

Following the promulgation of the First Ten Points, major attention was given in the mass media to discussions of how to implement two of the major policy guidelines which had been raised in that document: the establishment of peasant organizations, and the systematization of cadre participation in collective labor. A campaign was launched to establish "poor peasants' representative groups" (p'in-nung tai-piao hsiao-tsu) throughout the countryside. The responsibilities of these groups were defined as follows:

---

[20] *Ibid.*, Article VII.
[21] *Ibid.*, Article IX.
[22] *Ibid.*, Article IX.
[23] *Ibid.*, Article X.

16

. . . . to act as the assistant to the management committee of the production team; under the leadership of the Party, to conduct class education and education in Party policy among the poor and lower-middle peasants as well as the broad masses of commune members; to raise the ideological consciousness of the poor and lower-middle peasants; to consolidate the collective economy; and to take the lead in accomplishing various production tasks.[24]

The urgency of the need for strengthening the role of poor and lower-middle peasants in the production teams was indicated by the assertion that "in those production teams where leadership is held by upper-middle peasants, spontaneous capitalist influences will emerge . . . . leadership is likely to be usurped by the landlords and rich peasants."[25] As for the relationship between poor peasant representative groups and the Party branches within the production brigades, little was said except for the injunction for Party branches to "rely on such organizations, listen to what they say in their work, win their assistance, submit to their supervision, and organize the poor and lower-middle peasants through them."[26]

At the same time that the organizational activities of the poor and lower-middle peasants were being publicized, a series of "talks on cadres participating in collective productive labor" was initiated in the official *Jen-min Jih-pao*. These talks reiterated the demand of the First Ten Points that regular participation in labor by cadres was necessary both to guarantee sound direction of production and to prevent the alienation of the cadres from the masses.[27]

A need was seen to resolve the contradiction between "labor" *(lao-tung)* [direct engagement in the production process] and "work" *(kung-tso)* [official administrative and leadership responsibilities]. In order to free the cadres for greater participation in the former, officials at all levels were urged to hold fewer meetings and conferences, reduce the number and length of their official reports, and spend less time compiling statistics. Complaints about the heavy administrative burdens on cadres

---

[24] *Nan-fang Jih-pao* (Southern Daily) [hereafter NFJP] Canton, May 25, 1963. On the question of the composition of these peasants' groups, it was held that their members should be recruited and elected "according to democratic procedures by the poor and lower-middle peasants." It was not specified whether lower-middle peasants were eligible for election to these bodies or whether they were merely permitted to vote on name lists of candidates selected from among the poor peasants. Frequent references to "poor peasant representatives" without similar mention of lower-middle peasant members would seem to indicate that the latter were largely excluded from participating in these bodies. This was ostensibly a reversal from the First Ten Points, which had held that both poor and lower-middle peasants were eligible for election to peasants' committees. The stipulations of the First Ten Points on this matter, however, were later upheld by the September 1963 Policy Formulations. See Appendix C, Article IV.

[25] *NFJP,* August 24, 1963.

[26] *NFJP,* May 28, 1963.

[27] *JMJP,* May 20 and 25, 1963.

were met with the demand that the cadres improve their work methods so as to cut down on the amount of time spent in their offices.[28]

In July 1963, an entire issue of *Hung Ch'i* was devoted to an examination of the policy of cadres participating in labor, and to a review of experiences gained in various localities in implementing this policy. Cadre participation in labor was held to be the best method for raising the labor enthusiasm of the masses and for helping the cadres to rectify their own work styles and work methods. It was furthermore advocated as a means of "smashing and rooting out all kinds of reactionary forces which are trying vainly to erode and undermine the revolutionary dictatorship of the proletariat and the revolutionary party of the proletariat in our country."[29] The system of cadres participating in labor was thus seen as an instrument of class struggle against the subversive influences of the "four elements"—landlords, rich peasants, counter-revolutionaries, and bad elements.

In order to impel cadres to spend more time in production and less time in their offices, the total number of subsidized work-points *(pu-t'ieh kung-fen)* awarded to cadres for the fulfillment of nonproduction-related administrative tasks was generally reduced to the equivalent of one or two percent of the total annual work points of the production team or brigade.[30] In view of the fact that it had previously been a common practice among cadres to claim four percent (or, in some extreme cases, as much as ten percent) of the total work points of a team or brigade as their "fixed subsidy," this meant that many cadres would now have to spend more time in the fields, earning work points as ordinary laborers, in order to maintain their previous level of income. If this measure was not sufficiently compelling, a second system was adopted on an experimental basis in many areas whereby a minimum quota of labor days was fixed for cadres at each level from the hsien to the production team. These quotas varied from place to place, but a common practice was to fix the number of mandatory labor days for hsien cadres at 60 days per year, commune cadres at 120 days, and brigade level cadres at 180 days.[31] The twin systems of fixing minimum labor-day quotas and maximum limits on the number of subsidized work points for cadres together comprised the essence of the policy of "three fixes" *(san ting)* which was later universally adopted throughout the cities and countryside.

One of the first significant public references to the launching of a nationwide Socialist Education Movement came on July 1, 1963, when T'ao Chu, then First Secretary of the CCP South-Central Bureau, addressed a convocation of Party members in Canton:

---

[28] See, for example, *JMJP,* June 2, 4, and 18, 1963.

[29] *Hung Ch'i,* No. 13–14, 1963.

[30] *Ibid.*

[31] *Ibid.* These figures represent an average for the fourteen rural areas discussed by the editors of *Hung Ch'i.*

At the present time, it is necessary to hold high the three red banners of the general line, the great leap forward, and the people's communes, and, while accelerating the construction of socialism, launch a large-scale campaign for carrying out socialist education. This campaign will be of extreme importance and profound significance in guaranteeing our victory in the class struggle, the struggle for production, and scientific experimentation.[32]

It was against this background of intensified class organizational activities, stepped-up efforts at systematizing cadre participation in labor, and the start of public propaganda concerning the campaign that the second major socialist education directive was promulgated in September 1963.

---

[32] *NFJP*, July 2, 1963.

II
An Optimistic Definition

The summer of 1963 had been a period of testing. By September there had been four months of experimentation since the promulgation of the First Ten Points. Now the Central Committee issued a new directive—again in the form of ten points—which attempted to provide more detailed policy guidelines based on this experience. In the earlier document, the general work methods of the Movement had been left partially undefined. These were now spelled out more concretely. Entitled "Some Concrete Policy Formulations . . . . in the Rural Socialist Education Movement," this directive has now come to be known in Peking terminology as the Later Ten Points.[1] It is translated in full as Appendix C.

The importance attached to involving leadership personnel in the Movement was underlined by the call for all leading cadres, from provincial to hsien levels, personally to undertake "spot testing" (shih tien), join actively in the work at the basic levels, and not be satisfied with mere oral briefings and written reports. These officials, together with other outside personnel,[2] were to be grouped into "work teams" to carry

---

[1] In the accusations originating during the Cultural Revolution there has been some confusion in the use of the term "Later Ten Points." In one of the earliest official discussions (in June 1967) of the Socialist Education Movement documents, Peking referred only to the First Ten Points and the Twenty-three Articles. No mention was made of either a "Later Ten Points" or of a "Revised Draft of the Later Ten Points." However, vague references were made to the evil activities of Liu Shao-ch'i ("China's Khrushchev") during the latter part of 1964, i.e., about the time of the September 1964 document. (See Hung Ch'i, No. 10, 1967.) Unofficial sources were more explicit. Red Guard publications appeared which charged Liu with putting forward a "Later Ten Points" in 1964. Contributing to the confusion, these publications did not mention the existence of a September 1963 document. (See Ching-kang-shan, Peking, April 18, 1967, as translated in SCMP No. 3946, May 25, 1967, pp. 1–15; also Pa-i-san Hung-wei-ping, Tientsin, May 13, 1967, as translated in SCMM No. 583, July 10, 1967, pp. 24–30.) It was not until November 1967 that official sources first mentioned both the September 1963 and September 1964 documents (see JMJP, November 23, 1967, translated in Peking Review, No. 49, 1967). The September 1963 decision was now explicitly identified as the "Later Ten Points," and the September 1964 document as the "Revised Draft of the Later Ten Points." This terminology will be followed in this study.

[2] The document itself did not identify the types of people who were to participate in the work teams alongside the leading cadres. However, there is evidence to indicate that lower ranking personnel in Party and government offices, urban intellectuals, and students all played significant roles in socialist education work teams. See, for example, Harald Munthe-Kaas, "China's 'Four Cleanups'," Far Eastern Economic Review, June 9, 1966. Our own interviews with persons connected with the work team movement have tended to confirm Mr. Munthe-Kaas' analysis.

out intensive socialist education work for three months in a limited number of communes and/or production brigades selected by the Party for spot testing. The process of recruiting personnel for these work teams was not discussed except for the stipulations that there must be a careful screening of members to ban "unclean elements," and that an effort should be made to recruit cadres with experience in Party work. The size of the work teams was not indicated.[3] It was clear that the work teams were expected to play a guiding role. The precise relationship between these outside teams and the existing basic-level organs was, however, left ambiguous.

> In the Socialist Education Movement, it would obviously be wrong for the work teams to work in circles within the basic cadres . . . . without making contact and taking deep root among . . . . the poor and lower-middle peasant masses. However it would be equally wrong for them to brush aside the basic organizations and existing cadres, instead of carrying out work by relying upon them. This method of doing things would create an opposition between the basic-level cadres on the one hand, and the work team and poor and lower-middle peasants on the other, thereby undermining the smooth development of the movement.[4]

The warning to the work teams implied here—that they must not undermine the authority of the existing power structure in the countryside— was further reflected in the description of the relationship between work team personnel and basic-level cadres. The work teams were to be the "staff" of the basic-level cadres and were strictly to avoid monopolizing the functions of the latter. Yet at the same time they were instructed to draw up plans and "enlighten the basic cadres in the analysis of problems and the determination of policies and methods."[5]

Although rural Party organizations were not peremptorily to be shoved aside, an important component of the Movement as outlined in the Later Ten Points was the call for a readjustment of basic-level Party units, basic organs of the Youth League, Women's Associations, and militia, as well as of the commune and brigade structures. In addition to strengthening political education and organizational life, this readjustment was also to include: examination of each member's social background, political attitudes, and work performance; weeding out of degenerate elements; and strengthening of a "leadership nucleus" (ling-tao ho-hsin)

---

[3] According to an informant who played a leading role in the work team movement in Kwangtung province in 1964–1965, each work team consisted of about 100 members, under the overall direction of a leading cadre from the hsien level or above. Each team, in turn, was broken down into several "work groups" of about ten members. These small groups were then dispatched to individual production brigades, where they carried on the work of investigation and supervision.

[4] Appendix C, Article II.

[5] Ibid.

through cultivation of activist elements. In places where leadership in these organizations had been "usurped by the class enemy," work teams could be empowered to replace the "rotten" units.[6]

The stipulations for dealing with errant cadres clearly indicated, however, that the overall assessment of the cadre problem remained as it had been in May. Cadre errors were asserted to be "mostly limited to such common mistakes as excessive eating, excessive possessions, and petty theft."[7] Persuasive education, with the goal of "treating the illness to save the man," was still prescribed for these non-antagonistic contradictions. Work teams were particularly urged to avoid the error of "exaggerating the enemy's strength, forming a bad opinion of basic-level cadres and even regarding them as the major targets for our blows."[8] Even those cadres who had formed connections with class enemies were regarded as being qualitatively different from the class enemies themselves. They were to be dealt with by education, reform and consolidation. Most cases of disciplinary action against cadres would be handled during the latter stages of the movement "when the leadership and the masses have comparatively cooled off."[9]

A similarly optimistic assessment was reflected in those sections of the Later Ten Points which dealt with the peasant masses. This document, for the first time since the initiation of the Socialist Education Movement, provided a detailed discussion of class definitions among the peasantry. Major emphasis was placed on drawing correct distinctions between the three types of middle peasants: lower, common, and upper; and on establishing appropriate guidelines for dealing with the sons and daughters of landlords and rich peasants.

As for the upper-middle peasants, the need was stressed for gentle handling to avoid pushing them over to the side of the landlords, and to prevent an erosion of confidence on the part of the other middle peasants. Despite their "wavering attitude," the majority of upper-middle peasants were held to be "laborers and our friends," capable of following the socialist road. Firm but patient criticism and education, rather than struggle and coercion, were the methods to be used in consolidating the upper-middle peasants.[10]

In the case of children of landlord and rich peasant families, the majority were held to have never directly participated in exploitation and were expressly included in the 95 percent of the masses who were to be "won over" during the Socialist Education Movement.[11] The overall leniency prescribed in the treatment of middle peasants and children of land-

---

[6] *Ibid.*
[7] *Ibid.*, Article VI(1).
[8] *Ibid.*
[9] *Ibid.*
[10] *Ibid.*, Article V.
[11] *Ibid.*, Article X.

lords and rich peasants was further reflected in the assertion that even the great majority of the "four elements" who had engaged in sabotaging activities could be reformed by the awakened masses through the adoption of correct methods.[12]

In sum, after a summer of experimentation, the Later Ten Points reinforced the impressions derived from the First Ten Points: that the Movement would be relatively mild; and that the Party leadership was optimistic about its prospects for success. The target for nationwide completion of the Movement was, if anything, slightly reduced: it was now set at two to three years.[13]

Following the September directive, systems of regulating participation in labor were revised and codified for cadres at all levels. Cadres at the hsien level were now instructed to devote a minimum of one-third of their time, i.e., over 100 days per year, to physical labor (compared with an earlier average quota of 60 days); commune-level cadres were also required to spend upwards of 100 days in production (compared with 120 days); and brigade-level cadres were to labor for 150 to 200 days (compared with 180 days).[14] The most significant change in the new policy was the substantial increase in the labor quotas of cadres at the hsien level—earlier labor norms for the lower levels were either held unchanged or somewhat reduced. The main thrust of this revision was to increase on-the-spot, personal leadership at the basic levels by cadres above the commune level.

In the fall of 1963, in a further effort to strengthen personal leadership by higher officials, emphasis was placed upon the practice of "squatting at points" *(tun tien)*. This was held to be an effective means both of participating in labor and of conducting socialist education work among the cadres and masses. Assertedly, the work of many higher level cadres sent to the countryside in the past had been superficial and unsystematic. To remedy this, leading cadres were now expected to "show resolution in grasping work at individual points."[15] What this meant in practice was that instead of wandering about aimlessly, briefly supervising production here and holding a meeting there, these leading cadres were to take charge of the work teams and stay within a single production brigade for a "suitable length of time" so as to "grasp the work from beginning to end in the light of concrete conditions."[16] The overall significance of this method was explained in the following terms:

> Since a person's understanding always proceeds from the particular to the general, cadres who have stayed at specific points find it

---

[12] *Ibid.,* Article IX.
[13] *Ibid.,* Article I.
[14] *NFJP,* October 7, 1963.
[15] *JMJP,* November 7, 1963.
[16] *JMJP,* October 13 and 29, 1963; also *NFJP,* November 26 and December 7, 1963.

possible to understand things better, and to correctly grasp and analyze the overall situation. . . . By employing the method of using selected points for trial experiments before gradual popularization, they have been able to guide effectively the work of the entire commune. . . . Secondly, by staying regularly at specific points and doing labor there, they have proved in a very convincing way that our leading organs are not "bureaucratic establishments," but are offices where servants of the people perform revolutionary work. This will inevitably promote better relations between the higher and lower levels [of leadership] as well as between the cadres and the masses. . . .[17]

It was further held that, since "only a *small number* of cadres are presently able to understand the question of cadres participating in labor *from the angle of ideological revolution and class struggle*," primary emphasis should be given to "socialist education with class education as its main content."[18]

Also important, as we have seen, was the injunction that leading cadres must refrain from "taking over" from lower-level cadres while staying at a point. As one Party secretary reported:

. . . . When at first our cadres went out to production teams to work, they did not pay any attention to giving play to the role of the team cadres, and even concerned themselves with supervising details "as small as a sesame seed." As a result, not only did they fail to take part in labor, but they also fostered the idea of "depending on others" on the part of team cadres. Later, this method of monopolizing work and taking over work from others was changed, and more time has become available to cadres to participate in labor.[19]

On the question of the relationship between methods of participating in productive labor and methods of conducting socialist education work, the key link once again was to be the adoption by cadres of a "firm class standpoint." Through systematic observation and experimentation while participating in labor, cadres were expected to learn to distinguish between, on one side, "legitimate" family sideline occupations, trading activities in the rural fairs, small-scale peddling activities and temporary transport and marketing business done by commune members, and on the other, "serious" capitalist tendencies, speculations, and market-disturbing activities of bad elements.[20]

In drawing such distinctions, and in restating this traditional class line of relying on the poor and lower-middle peasants, uniting the middle peasants, and winning over all who could be won over (including the ab-

---

[17] *NFJP*, November 26, 1963; see also *Union Research Service* (Hong Kong, Union Research Institute) Vol. 36, No. 15 (August 21, 1964).

[18] *JMJP*, October 8 and November 29, 1963 (emphasis added).

[19] *Ibid.*, October 8, 1963.

[20] *NFJP*, December 14, 1963.

solute majority of upper-middle peasants), the Party hoped to strengthen the collectivist component of agricultural production and marketing activities, while also drawing a clear line of demarcation between friends and enemies. At the same time, however, an explicit injunction prohibited use of "struggle" in all but "a very small number" of serious cases involving conscious and active attempts to undermine the interests of state, collective, and masses. This caveat was intended to prevent the alienation of the majority of upper-middle peasants who, though having capitalist tendencies, had demonstrated superior qualities as producers.[21]

The dilemma faced by Party leaders in attempting to ensure that intensified class education would not adversely affect production was also manifested in periodic reminders to cadres that socialist education work must be "strictly coordinated with production."[22] Despite the confident claim that "once class struggle is grasped, miracles are possible," *(chieh-chi tou-cheng i chua chiu ling)*[23] the ambivalence of concrete policies indicated the existence of substantial limitations on the problem-solving potential of class struggle.

Such limitations notwithstanding, the official *Jen-min Jih-pao* New Year editorial for 1964 expressed optimism in its assessment of developments during 1963 and in its call to push the Socialist Education Movement forward with even greater vigor in 1964:

> Over the past year, the widespread unfolding of the Socialist Education Movement throughout the urban and rural areas was an historically significant movement of ideological revolution which took class education as its main content and which was self-consciously participated in by countless masses of people. . . . Wherever the Socialist Education Movement has been launched, the socialist consciousness of the cadres and masses has been greatly elevated, and blows have been dealt to the remnants of capitalist forces and feudal forces. . . . This very good political situation is a decisive factor in promoting the beginning of an all-round turn for the better in our national economy.
>
> In the new year, we must carry forward the Socialist Education Movement in even greater depth and scope; we must carry it out phase by phase and group by group. Cadres at all levels throughout the whole country must participate in this movement in an organized and planned manner, on the one hand helping basic-level units to carry out their work, and on the other hand receiving education along with the broad masses. . . .[24]

---

21 *Ibid.*

22 See, for example, *NFJP*, December 28, 1963.

23 *JMJP*, November 29, 1963.

24 *JMJP*, January 1, 1964. The phrase "countless masses of people" *(i wan ch'ün-chung)*, as used in the opening sentence of this editorial, has often been erroneously (though perhaps more literally) translated as "hundreds of millions of people," thus leading to an exaggerated view of the overall dimensions of the Socialist Education Movement in 1963. The term is generally used in a hyperbolic sense to imply vastness rather than a specific number.

The year 1964 was a year in which "politics took command" throughout China. It was in 1964 that the People's Liberation Army was held up as a model of political and ideological virtue for the whole nation to emulate, that the cry went out to "cultivate actively the revolutionary successor generation," that the campaign of vilification against Soviet "revisionism" reached fever pitch, and that the cult of "Mao-study" began to be propagated on a nationwide basis.[25] In line with these developments, the Socialist Education Movement left the experimental stage in 1964 to become a full-blown mass movement.

The economic situation in China was somewhat brighter at the beginning of 1964 than it had been a year earlier. There had been further gains in the recovery from the "three lean years." This fact undoubtedly influenced Party leaders in their decision to step up the tempo of the Socialist Education Movement. This decision was not, however, based on the type of euphoria which had been so prevalent in the fall of 1958 when the communes were first launched on a nationwide scale. It was a reasonably optimistic assessment of rural conditions in general, and of the basic health and vitality of the communes in particular, that in 1964 enabled Party leaders confidently to "unfold the class struggle" in the countryside. Problems, to be sure, existed. Particularly, as we have seen, these were among the cadres at both higher and lower levels. But on the whole, the Socialist Education Movement was viewed by the regime as a sign of health rather than disease, an invigorating tonic rather than a violent purgative.[26]

Various methods were used to implement the campaign in the first half of 1964. Most of these had by this time become standard techniques of education and indoctrination. Among the most favored were: "recall the past" meetings; compilation by peasants of the "three histories" (personal, family, and village); organization and consolidation of poor and lower-middle peasant groups; and a general campaign by cadres to "talk about, demonstrate, discuss, record, and spread" the lessons of class education and class struggle among the peasantry. In addition, the movement to "study, compare, and catch up with the advanced and help the backward" was stressed as a means of strengthening brigades and teams which were lagging behind in production. Systems of regulating cadre participation in labor were also normalized with the universal adoption of the "three fixes": fixed labor norms, fixed work posts, and fixed workpoint subsidies.[27]

---

[25] For a brief summary and analysis of these developments, see Richard Baum, "Ideology Redivivus," *Problems of Communism* Vol. XVI (May–June 1967) pp. 1–11.

[26] See, for example, T'ao Chu, "The People's Communes Forge Ahead," *Peking Review* Nos. 13 and 15, 1964.

[27] For materials relating to these developments, see *Jen-min Shou-ts'e* (People's Handbook) Peking: 1964, pp. 78–87, 88–96, 291–96, 566–90, and *passim*.

In June 1964, at a Work Conference of the Standing Committee of the CCP Politburo, Mao Tse-tung personally laid down "six criteria" for evaluating the success or failure of the Socialist Education Movement. In the order of presentation, these were:

1) Have the poor and lower-middle peasants been truly mobilized?
2) Has the problem of the Four Uncleans among the cadres been resolved?
3) Have the cadres participated in physical labor?
4) Has a good leadership nucleus been established?
5) When landlords, rich peasants, counter-revolutionaries and bad elements who engage in destructive activities are discovered, is this contradiction merely turned over to the higher levels, or are the masses mobilized to supervise strictly, criticize, and even appropriately struggle against these elements, and moreover to retain them for reform on the spot?
6) Is production increasing or decreasing?[28]

Little is known about the Work Conference which brought forth these six criteria. But in June 1964, the Party also issued an eighteen point Organizational Rules of Poor and Lower-Middle Peasant Associations.[29] In giving concrete form to the peasant organizations which had been called for since May 1963, these Organizational Rules settled some issues which had previously been left open.[30] The fundamental ambiguity of the associations' role was not, however, fully resolved. An example of this was the attempt to prevent conflicts of interest from arising, and to strengthen the supervisory role of the peasant associations. Leading members of the associations were expressly prohibited from serving concurrently in such posts as commune, production brigade or team leader, accountant or cashier, custodian, or manager of commune or brigade-run enterprises and sideline occupations.[31] This bolstered the peasants' power to "supervise the work of management committees at each level." On the other hand, the independence of the peasants' associations was sharply circumscribed by the requirement that they strictly follow the leadership of the basic-level Party organizations.[32] Thus, despite an explicit grant of

---

[28] References to Mao's authorship of the "six criteria" are contained in both the Revised Later Ten Points of September 1964 (see Appendix E) and the Twenty-three Articles of January 1965 (see Appendix F).

[29] See Appendix D.

[30] For example, in addition to the question of concurrent posts discussed below, the September 1963 decision had also listed as "problems remaining to be solved" the following: the names of the peasants' organizations; their tasks and powers; whether the basic unit should be the production brigade or production team; their relationship to Party organizations and management committees; whether they should be established at the hsien level; and whether regular representatives' meetings should be held at the provincial level. These questions were either fully or partially discussed in the Organizational Rules of June 1964.

[31] Appendix D, Article VIII.

[32] *Ibid.*, Introductory section and Article IX.

authority to the peasants to assist management committees and control organs in carrying out the work of the Four Cleans, and despite a stern prohibition against cadres "striking retaliatory blows" against those peasants who might criticize them, the scope of the poor and lower-middle peasants' mandate was by no means clear.

Following the June Work Conference and the promulgation of the Organizational Rules, enthusiastic reports on the progress of the Socialist Education Movement in the countryside poured in from all parts of the nation. A few samples from provincial radio broadcasts of the period will serve to convey this dominantly enthusiastic mood:

> Since the beginning of June, cadres at all levels have gone to production teams to launch the masses, to display successes, and to discover problems. . . . Poor and lower-middle peasants are actively taking the lead in this campaign. . . .[33]
> . . . . As a result of the Socialist Education Movement, the cadres now have clearer views about relying on the poor and lower-middle peasants, and can carry out Party policies and principles better. . . . Party members have also improved their work styles, taken an active part in collective labor, and are selfless and public spirited. . . .[34]
> . . . . By going out into the fields to carry out on-the-spot checks, brigade and team cadres . . . . got rid of complacency and lethargy. . . . . Everyone cleared their heads, and the masses were mobilized. . . .[35]

In the summer of 1964 the Socialist Education Movement seemed to be proceeding smoothly and on course. In retrospect, however, this now appears to have been merely a calm before the proverbial storm. The first concrete indications of the coming storm appeared in September 1964 with the promulgation of the Revised Draft of the Later Ten Points.

---

[33] *Radio Changsha* (Hunan), June 27, 1964.
[34] *Radio Wuhan* (Hupeh), July 1, 1964.
[35] *Radio Hangchow* (Chekiang), September 7, 1964.

III
A Pessimistic Reformulation

The Revised Draft of the Later Ten Points, as might be expected, had many similarities to the original version of the Later Ten Points. Many sections of the earlier document were reproduced verbatim or with but minor change. The fundamental tone, however, was quite different. The relatively sanguine view of September 1963—which had continued to be expressed as late as mid-1964—was now replaced by a markedly pessimistic outlook. The seriousness with which problems in the country-side were being viewed in September 1964 was indicated at the outset of the Revised Later Ten Points by the altered estimate that completion of the Socialist Education Movement would require five to six years— or even longer.[1]

The new mood was also reflected in a change of emphasis concerning work methods. Although in broad terms there were no new methods introduced, the elaboration of previously advocated methods indicated significant differences. For example, whereas the September 1963 version had called for the work of personal "spot testing" by leading cadres to be completed within a period of three months, the Revised Later Ten Points specifically stated that such work (now referred to as "squatting at a point") would require about six months.[2] New emphasis was also placed on the need to have "staunch" work teams led by "politically strong and capable persons," and the status of such outside working personnel was correspondingly upgraded. All provinces and municipalities were instructed to organize a number of "specialized work teams" to play leading roles in the movement.[3]

This stress on the need to strengthen rural leadership with outside personnel from higher levels was accompanied by clear evidence of increasing disillusionment with the quality of existing basic-level organizations. The September 1963 injunction against "brushing aside" basic-level cadres was deleted. Instead, the Revised Later Ten Points warned:

> [If] the work team concerns itself only with activity among basic-level cadres . . . . it will be "much ado about nothing" for a few people. Thus the movement will end in failure or reap very negligible results, and the consequences may be quite serious.[4]

---

[1] See Appendix E, Article I.

[2] *Ibid.*, Article II.

[3] *Ibid.*

[4] *Ibid.* Compare this statement to the warning in the September 1963 formulation against "brushing aside" the basic-level cadres: see Appendix C, Article II (4).

In addition to this admonition about the danger of superficiality in Four Cleans work, stress was given in the new directive to the need for recruiting activist elements into basic-level organs of the Party. Moreover, a new registration of Party members was called for—a step which had been left undecided a year before.[5]

Few changes were called for in the policy for dealing with middle peasants and the offspring of landlords and rich peasants, but there were several indications in the new directive that a hardening of class lines in dealing with the masses was intended. A section of the Later Ten Points which warned against subjecting the upper-middle peasants to excessive struggle was now deleted.[6] The Later Ten Points had also stated that the concern with class definitions did not mean that there would be a new division of classes in the countryside.[7] The Revised Later Ten Points, however, clearly foreshadowed such a step: it called for the first general reclassification since the Land Reform of 1949–52:

> Since there is widespread confusion about class background in the villages it is necessary to clearly define class ranks as a part of the work of the Socialist Education Movement. The background of each rural household should be examined and classified after full discussion by the masses, and a class file should be established.[8]

Undoubtedly the most significant part of this September 1964 assessment of rural conditions dealt with the basic-level cadres. A year earlier, the most prevalent cadre mistakes had been treated as petty corruption. The Revised Later Ten Points now saw the situation in a much more serious light:

> [The basic-level rural cadres] have not only committed the "four uncleans" economically, but have also failed to draw the line between friend and enemy, lost their own stand, discriminated against poor and lower-middle peasants, hid their backgrounds and fabricated history, and so forth, thus committing "four uncleans" politically and organizationally. . . . Some have even degenerated into agents and protectors of class enemies. . . . The problem, as we can see, is indeed serious.[9]

Some by now almost standard statements about the cadres were repeated. The majority at the basic-level were basically good. By persuasion and education, 95 percent of them could be consolidated. And, as in the Later Ten Points, two principal deviations in this work were criticized: on one hand, an overly lenient and superficial handling of cadre mistakes;

---

[5] Appendix E, Article VIII.
[6] The Revised Later Ten Points retained, instead, a more general injunction against using coercion in dealing with the upper-middle peasants
[7] Appendix C, introductory section.
[8] Appendix E, Article V.
[9] *Ibid.*, Article VI.

on the other, an excessive "dealing of blows." But where the 1963 directive had seen the excessive dealing of blows as the more harmful, the September 1964 revised version reversed this order and announced that lenient and superficial handling of cadre mistakes was the more dangerous tendency.[10] A new method of handling the basic-level cadres was now required if their more serious errors were not to avoid detection or be treated superficially. This method was referred to in the Revised Later Ten Points as the "bold mobilization of the masses":

> Among all work items of the Socialist Education Movement, mobilization of the masses should be put in the first place. It is the fundamental task in developing the Socialist Education Movement. . . . . Some cadres are hesitant in mobilizing the masses. . . . Other cadres are opposed [to it]. . . . They are all very wrong. . . . All those who have a wavering attitude toward the Socialist Education Movement first waver on the question of mobilizing the masses. All those who oppose the Socialist Education Movement first oppose mobilizing the masses.[11]

Although mobilization of the masses had been a frequent call prior to the Revised Later Ten Points, it now took on a more ominous meaning as far as the cadres were concerned. This can be seen in a section of the directive devoted to criticism of past performance:

> During the Four Cleans movement, because of fear of "hurting the cadres' feelings," or of [adversely] affecting the unity of the cadres, or of the cadres' quitting work, the work teams in some places assumed a tolerant attitude toward cadres who had committed even serious mistakes. They were afraid to criticize, to engage in struggle and especially to mobilize the masses. . . . They thought . . . . they had achieved unity. Yet the result was they were . . . . divorced from the masses and achieved only a superficial, temporary and false consolidation.[12]

Thus previous restraints against attacking basic-level cadres were significantly attenuated, if not largely removed. The September 1963 concern with preventing a serious weakening of the authority of existing basic-level organizations and cadres was no longer articulated. But if the basic-level cadres were now to face the storm, the Revised Later Ten Points indicated that they might not be alone:

> Experience . . . . has revealed that cadres in basic-level organizations who have committed serious mistakes are usually connected with

---

[10] *Ibid.*

[11] *Ibid.*, Article II(4). As if to emphasize the new pessimistic assessment of the basic-level cadres, the Revised Later Ten Points stated that the majority of cadres could be consolidated only *after* the peasant masses had been fully mobilized—a clear reversal of priorities from the September 1963 document. Compare Appendix C, Article VI, with Appendix E, Article VI.

[12] Appendix E, Article VI (2).

certain cadres of higher level organizations . . . . and are instigated, supported and protected by them. In such cases we must go to the origin and get hold of the responsible persons. No matter to what level the cadres belong, or what positions they hold, ... they should be subjected to open criticism before the people. . . .[13]

The implications of this allegation concerning the existence of higher level supporters and instigators of aberrant cadres were not, however, immediately apparent in September of 1964. Indeed, it was not until the promulgation of the Twenty-three Articles some four months later that this became a significant issue in the Socialist Education Movement.

In the months following the adoption of the Revised Later Ten Points, the poor and lower-middle peasants were exhorted to strengthen their supervision *(chien-tu)* over those basic-level cadres who had been guilty of the Four Uncleans. According to *Jen-min Jih-pao:* "no major problems in the countryside can be resolved without the consent of the peasant associations. They must dare to supervise the cadres, dare to attack the enemy, and dare to oppose all bad people and bad things."[14]

This was not, to be sure, a radically new departure. A similar injunction had appeared in the June 1964 peasant association regulations. But in the intervening four months the dominant mood had changed from optimism to caution, and finally to deep concern over the performance of the basic-level rural cadres. In response to this new mood, the official invitation to poor and lower-middle peasants to "dare to supervise the cadres" was taken up with a vengeance.

One of the earliest signs of the developing mass campaign of criticism against basic-level cadres was the publication of a letter from a poor peasant in Kwangtung province to the influential *Nan-fang Jih-pao.* After complaining about the prevalent cadre practice of awarding themselves excess work-points in the form of fixed subsidies, this peasant went on: "when you cadres are unfair, we will criticize and supervise you; if you do not accept our criticism . . . . we may fire you."[15] With the dikes thus opened, the flood waters were not long in coming.

Financial supervisory groups of poor and lower-middle peasants, acting with the express or implied consent of Party committees at the hsien and commune levels, soon uncovered numerous acts of misappropriation of public funds, acceptance of bribes, and personal extravagance on the part of basic-level cadres.[16] The most frequent accusation against the cadres concerned their methods of recording work-points. In what must have been a humiliating experience for the cadres, "distribution teams" of peasants seized the cadres' work-point handbooks and conducted de-

---

13 *Ibid.*
14 *JMJP,* October 29, 1964.
15 *NFJP,* October 11, 1964.
16 See, for example, *NFJP,* October 14, 1964.

tailed examinations of the records contained therein. The peasants found numerous instances of "secret subsidies," "nepotistic favoritism," and out-and-out "falsification of records." Often the cadres were discovered to have appropriated for themselves as fixed subsidies as much as four or five percent of the total work-points of a brigade or team, in disregard of the existing policy which had set the maximum for such subsidies at one to two percent.[17] In an article entitled "Cleaning-up Work Points and Cleaning-up Ideology," the editors of *Nan-fang Jih-pao* stated that the practice of cadres misappropriating work-points was anti-socialist and exploitative in nature, and should be "dug up at the roots."[18]

The besieged cadres attempted to fight back against their peasant detractors by claiming that "if the masses criticize the cadres, the cadres will not be able to lead them at all. It's all right for higher levels to criticize cadres, but if the masses do it, things will become chaotic."[19] A similar argument held that "we are relying too much on the poor and lower-middle peasants; it is not easy to do our work. . . . What's the use of having cadres if the peasants are going to run things?"[20] These views were strongly rebuked. As a warning to those cadres who might be tempted to "hit back" at their critics, *Jen-min Jih-pao* sternly announced that "the cadres must self-consciously and uninterruptedly accept supervision by their poor and lower-middle peasant brothers."[21]

In addition to being subjected to criticism, supervision, and even dismissal for their alleged work-point malfeasances, the rural cadres also came under fire for having allowed individual peasants to expand their private sideline occupations at the expense of collective undertakings, and for having failed to heed the regulation that private individuals working at sideline occupations should surrender their products to the collective in exchange for work-points.[22] As a result of such "willful negligence" on the part of cadres, peasants had been allowed to sell their sideline products for cash on the open market. According to one report from Kwangtung province, "many basic-level cadres and commune members thought that [collective] agricultural work was not as profitable as [private] cash undertakings, so they swarmed to the mountains to fell trees, leaving no labor force for planned work in collective fields."[23]

Not only were the cadres criticized for permitting such "spontaneous capitalist tendencies" to flourish; they were also publicly reprimanded for having aided the peasants in resisting the state plan for "unified purchase" of excess grain. Compulsory grain delivery quotas had been

---

[17] *Ibid.;* also *JMJP*, December 11, 1964.
[18] *NFJP*, December 26, 1968.
[19] *Radio Tientsin* (Hopeh), December 19, 1964.
[20] *Radio Nanchang* (Kiangsi), December 18, 1964.
[21] *JMJP*, December 4, 1964.
[22] *NFJP*, November 9, 1964.
[23] *Ibid.*

raised somewhat in late 1964, and some cadres assertedly had taken the position that "we have suffered severe natural disasters this year . . . . the masses have experienced much bitterness. It is not easy for them to harvest more food grain." Such opinions were condemned as manifestations of "a completely erroneous ideological tendency."[24] A second erroneous tendency with respect to the state plan for unified purchase was manifested by certain cadres in Hupeh province who were reported to have argued: "This food is what we have earned by our labor. It should be shared out according to the number of persons and be put at the disposal of individual team members." This latter argument was held to represent the capitalist position taken by class enemies, and was roundly criticized.[25]

Throughout the late fall of 1964 the cadres were thus attacked from all directions, and their modest efforts at self-defense were summarily dismissed as attempts to "hoodwink the masses." Clearly, the prestige and status of the basic-level cadres were being severely undermined, if not directly threatened.

The attack on the cadres was accompanied, however, by increasing signs of theoretical confusion. Petty corruption (most notably the misappropriation of work-points) which had previously been viewed as a *non*-antagonistic contradiction was now denounced as "anti-socialist" in nature.[26] The Revised Later Ten Points, without explicitly redefining the Four Cleans, had spoken harshly of the Four Uncleans in politics and organization, as well as in economics. This document had repeated much of the earlier language to the effect that the most important contradictions were those among the people. But it had also stated that the main objective was "the solution of the 'four uncleans' among the cadres *and the launching of the struggle against the enemy.*"[27] Thus the cadre problem had been expressly linked with an antagonistic contradiction. Shortly afterwards, however, *Jen-min Jih-pao,* in its National Day editorial of October 1st, said that "the great historical significance of the [Socialist Education] Movement lies in the following fact—it is a movement for educating the cadres and masses in the revolutionary spirit of the general line *and for correctly handling contradictions among the people.*"[28] Thus, by the late fall of 1964, there apparently existed some uncertainty as to both the basic nature of the cadre problem and the proper focus of socialist education work.

---

[24] See *Radio Wuhan* (Hupeh), November 10, 11, and 23, 1964; also *Radio Kunming* (Yunnan), November 11, 1964.
[25] *Radio Wuhan* (Hupeh), November 11, 1964.
[26] *NFJP,* December 26, 1964.
[27] Appendix E, Article I (emphasis added).
[28] *JMJP,* October 1, 1964 (emphasis added).

IV
An Attempt to Redefine the Goals

By the end of 1964 attempts were being made to remedy this theoretical confusion. Premier Chou En-lai, in his "Report on Government Work" to the National People's Congress on December 21–22, discussed basic guidelines for the Socialist Education Movement. Chou spoke of the need to undertake "cleaning up *(ch'ing-li)* and basic construction *(chi-pen chien-she)* in politics, economics, ideology, and organization."[1] This curious change in the terminology of the Four Cleans movement (to be officially ratified a month later in the Twenty-three Articles) implied a shift of emphasis away from the relatively narrow and concrete realm of squaring accounts, granaries, properties, and work points to the more inclusive goal of rectifying general social, political, and economic ideas and institutions.

Shortly after Chou's report was published, another significant statement bearing on the theoretical question of orientation appeared in the *Jen-min Jih-pao* New Year editorial for 1965. This statement not only failed to stress the line (articulated as late as October 1) that the main goal of the campaign was to educate the cadres and masses correctly to recognize and handle *non-antagonistic contradictions,* but on the contrary it asserted:

> The principal contradiction in China today is the [antagonistic] *contradiction between socialism and capitalism.* . . . The Socialist Education Movement now unfolding in the urban and rural areas is directed precisely at carrying further the resolution of this contradiction. . . . So long as we get a firm grasp of this contradiction . . . . we shall be able to promote socialism and eradicate capitalism.[2]

The theoretical reorientation of the Socialist Education Movement was carried a step further in mid-January of 1965 when a Work Conference of the Politburo (assertedly acting under the personal guidance of Mao Tse-tung) promulgated the celebrated twenty-three point directive, "Some Problems Currently Arising in the Course of the Rural Socialist Education Movement."

The Twenty-three Articles is certainly the most terse and obscure of the directives associated with the Socialist Education Movement.[3] It also

---

[1] *Jen-min Shou-ts'e,* 1965, pp. 9–16.
[2] *JMJP,* January 1, 1965.
[3] The Chinese text of the Twenty-three Articles has approximately 5,600 characters. This compares with approximately 10,000 characters in the First Ten Points, 19,000 in the Later Ten Points, and 20,000 in the Revised Later Ten Points.

clearly seems to have reflected a growing awareness of the necessity for a thorough reappraisal of the leadership and general orientation of the Movement. The primary question thus was quickly posed: What is the nature of the Movement? Three possible answers were offered. Two of these were rejected as "erroneous"; only one was "correct." The erroneous viewpoints were: 1) the Socialist Education Movement is mainly concerned with resolving the contradiction between the Four Cleans and the Four Uncleans in the conduct of basic-level cadres; and 2) the Movement involves an overlapping *(chiao ch'a)* of contradictions within the Party and contradictions outside of the Party, or between contradictions with the enemy and contradictions among the people. These viewpoints were both held to be "un-Marxist-Leninist" because they could be applied "to all political parties in all societies and at all historical periods." The only correct way to look at the Movement was in terms of the contradiction between socialism and capitalism. Only this latter interpretation was Marxist-Leninist; it alone was fully in accord with the "scientific theories" developed by Mao Tse-tung on the subject of continued class struggle during the transitional period from capitalism to socialism.[4]

In thus stressing antagonistic class contradictions as the main focus of future socialist education work, this formulation was consistent with the line which had been taken earlier in the *Jen-min Jih-pao* New Year editorial. It thus ostensibly helped to reduce the theoretical confusion over basic directions and guidelines which had been evident in the period after the promulgation of the Revised Later Ten Points. The *practical* implications of this "new line" were not, however, immediately apparent from the document itself. On one hand, by portraying the nature of the movement in the harshest possible theoretical terms as a struggle between socialism and capitalism, the Twenty-three Articles could readily be interpreted as a hardening of the Party's class line—and as a signal for more drastic measures against "spontaneous capitalist tendencies" in rural areas. On the other hand, however, the major focus of conflict in the countryside during the previous four months had been the basic level cadres' alleged Four Unclean acts of petty economic corruption, which had generally been viewed as a contradiction among the people. It is thus possible that in shifting the focus of the movement away from the resolution of the old Four Uncleans to the handling of more fundamental (and more abstract) contradictions *between the two roads,* the Twenty-three Articles were actually intended to ameliorate, rather than intensify, existing patterns of conflict in the countryside.[5]

---

4 Appendix F, Article II.

5 In this regard, it is interesting to note the charge against Liu Shao-ch'i and others which linked their alleged advocacy of the "two erroneous views" of the nature of the movement to the mistaken policy of excessive struggle against basic-level cadres. See *JMJP,* April 2, 1967.

Perhaps the most obvious indication that a serious attempt was being made to clarify the orientation of the Socialist Education Movement was the inclusion in the Twenty-three Articles of a new statement of basic aims for the Movement, a statement which has since been hailed by proponents of the cultural revolution as a major theoretical innovation by Mao Tse-tung:

> The key point of this Movement is to rectify *(cheng)* those people in positions of authority within the Party who take the capitalist road. . . . . Of these people . . . . some are out in the open and some remain concealed. Of the people who support them, some are at lower levels and some at higher levels. . . . Among those at higher levels, there are some people in the communes, districts, hsiens, special districts, *and even in the work of Provincial and Central Committee departments,* who oppose socialism.[6]

This statement is reminiscent of—though more explicit than—the reference in the Revised Later Ten Points to higher level "protectors" and "instigators" of wayward cadres. It may be interpreted as a further attempt to shift the focus of hostility away from the basic-level cadres. However, this is not entirely clear from the text itself, since the basic-level cadres (". . . . some are at lower levels") were at least implicitly included within the scope of the new statement as potential targets for future rectification.

The theoretical formulations raised in the Twenty-three Articles thus contained a certain amount of inherent ambiguity. Similarly, those sections of the document which dealt with concrete policy problems tended to indicate an indecisive blend of continuity with the past and subtle shifts of emphasis for the future. In terms of basic work methods, the importance of sending work teams of higher-level cadres to "squat at points" in the countryside was reaffirmed, with the added stipulation that leading personnel from the regional bureaus of the Party Central Committee would now participate in this program.[7] While the leading role of the work teams was thus reaffirmed, the previous requirement that all members of these teams be politically and ideologically "clean" was explicitly annulled by the Twenty-three Articles.[8]

An attempt was made to circumscribe the broad leadership mandate which had previously been given to the work teams. In order to prevent them from usurping authority in the production brigades and teams, warnings were now issued against the concentration of excessively large groups of outside personnel in a single production brigade or team, and

---

[6] Appendix F, Article II (emphasis added).

[7] *Ibid.,* Article VII.

[8] *Ibid.,* Article XIV. This article stipulates that persons who have committed mistakes may participate in work teams in order to promote their own education and transformation.

against reliance on "human wave tactics" in carrying out the Movement.[9] Moreover, a new call was issued for the establishment of "three-way alliances" *(san chieh-ho)* among peasants, basic-level cadres, and work teams.[10]

The basic-level cadres were viewed with less suspicion and distrust in the Twenty-three Articles than had been the case in the Revised Later Ten Points. Although severe disciplinary measures were sanctioned in the most serious cases of violations of law by the cadres, the main emphasis was once again on education and persuasion. Work teams and other authoritative organs in the countryside were instructed to be very careful in classifying basic-level cadres, so as to draw a clear distinction between the vast majority of cadres who could be "transformed" and the very few who had to be "struggled against," fired from their posts, or even arrested.[11]

The need to mobilize the masses was reasserted in the Twenty-three Articles, but a new warning against "going too far" was added:

> We must boldly unleash the masses; we must not be like women with bound feet. . . . At the same time . . . . we must eliminate simple, crude work methods, severely prohibit beating people and other forms of physical punishment, and prevent forced confessions.[12]

Although the Twenty-three Articles portrayed an overall situation in the countryside somewhat brighter than that depicted in the Revised Later Ten Points, there was no indication of a return to the optimism of mid-1964. The Socialist Education Movement was viewed as a long-term, serious process which would require six or seven years for completion.[13]

On the whole, the Twenty-three Articles, while toning down the generally bleak outlook and the harshness of disciplinary measures against the cadres which had characterized the previous period, was not wholly unequivocal in its formulation of new goals and directions. Despite the visible attempt to establish a new overall policy line, the document was largely phrased in terms of formulas and prescriptions which had previously appeared in one or more of the earlier directives, albeit the "mix" was now somewhat different and new emphases and nuances of meaning had been added.[14] Many of the crucial issues of the Socialist

---

[9] *Ibid.*, Article VI. Limiting the size of the work teams was said to be advantageous because, in addition to making it possible to deal with more "points" simultaneously, it was also "beneficial to taking the mass line."

[10] *Ibid.*, Article V.

[11] *Ibid.*, Articles V and IX.

[12] *Ibid.*, Article V.

[13] *Ibid.*, Article XI.

[14] The Twenty-three Articles did not, as now claimed by Peking, directly repudiate the Revised Later Ten Points. Note, for instance, the injunction in Article I that the whole Party should actively and resolutely "continue to execute the Central Committee's various decisions [sic] concerning the Socialist Education Movement."

38

Education Movement were thus left either unclearly defined or cloaked in generalities.

Whatever the ambiguities of the Twenty-three Articles, there soon seemed to be a shift in the orientation of cadre policy. Up to the eve of the Politburo Work Conference (in mid-January, 1965), the Chinese press and radio had carried reports of peasant criticism of cadre corruption. They now fell largely silent on this subject.[15]

As the Socialist Education Movement developed in the spring and summer of 1965, the consolidation of cadres and masses once again became a major focus. Mild methods for persuasion of cadres were advocated. It was noted that many cadres, having been severely criticized by the masses and work teams in recent months, had become passive in their work for fear of committing further mistakes.[16] There was little evidence, however, that this easing of pressure on the basic-level cadres was accompanied by any major shift of the Four Cleans movement to new targets at higher levels.[17]

Although the quest for unity among cadres and masses was the core of the new orientation in rural policy, there was no corresponding diminution of exhortations to "boldly mobilize the masses"; nor was there any apparent reduction of the supervisory powers of the peasant organizations. Instead, a major theme of the many provincial poor and lower-middle peasant congresses held in the first half of 1965 was that the poor and lower-middle peasants should be "masters of their own house" in leading class struggle and the battle for production.[18]

---

[15] See, for example, *Radio Taiyuan* (Shansi), January 7, 1965; also *Radio Wuhan* (Hupeh), January 10, 1965; and *Radio Nanning* (Kwangsi), January 12, 1965. In the months following the promulgation of the Twenty-three Articles there were no references to cadre corruption in official media sources. Indeed, the only reference the authors have been able to find was one which appeared in the Hong Kong *Sing Tao Daily News* of March 6, alluding to complaints of cadre corruption in certain rural areas of Kwangtung province.

[16] See, for example, *Radio Sian* (Shensi), February 24, 1965.

[17] Only at the provincial level and above does sufficient personnel data exist to make it possible to determine, in the absence of direct information, whether or not extensive purging occurred. In 1965, aside from such presumably unrelated organs as the Ministry of Culture, there was official confirmation of an extensive personnel shakeup only in Kweichow province. See Frederick C. Teiwes, *Provincial Party Personnel in Mainland China 1956–1966* (New York: Columbia University, East Asian Institute, 1967) p. 35. During the Cultural Revolution this shakeup has been explicitly linked to the Four Cleans movement: see, for example, *Radio Kweiyang* (Kweichow), June 3, 1967. There have been, in addition, some unconfirmed reports by refugees and foreign residents in China that some purging at the commune level did occur in 1965, although the extent of this purging cannot, at this time, be determined. See, for example, Ray Wylie, "Struggle at Horse Bridge," *Far Eastern Economic Review,* August 31, 1967.

[18] See, for example, Liu Chien-hsün's speech to the Honan Provincial Congress of Poor and Lower-middle Peasants and Advanced Producers, *Radio Chengchow* (Honan), May 4, 1965.

In May 1965, *Jen-min Jih-pao* bluntly declared an expansion of the targets of class struggle:

In the course of the struggle between the two roads of socialism and capitalism in the countryside, there are contradictions between the enemy and ourselves as well as contradictions among the people. The former should be emphasized, while the latter should not be overlooked. . . . At present, some people think that class struggle is confined solely to the struggle against the restorative activities of landlords, rich peasants, counter-revolutionaries, and other reactionary forces. This reduces the scope of class struggle. *We should make it clear that in the countryside, an important aspect of the struggle between two roads is the struggle between the socialist direction of the poor and lower-middle peasants and the capitalist tendencies of the upper-middle peasants. . . .*[19]

The class line in the countryside was thus revised so as to include not only the open restorative activities of the "four elements," but also the more "spontaneous" (and less easily detectable) capitalist tendencies of the upper-middle peasants under the rubric of antagonistic class contradictions.

It was apparent, nonetheless, that the precise point at which private economic activities ceased being legitimate livelihood pursuits—and became antagonistic class contradictions—proved elusive. Great numbers of letters began to pour in to newspapers and magazines from readers in all parts of the country requesting clarification concerning identification and classification of "spontaneous capitalist tendencies." One of the topics most frequently raised in these letters was the question of differentiating between legitimate sideline occupations and those which were capitalist-leaning. The official response to such questions indicated that many work teams and cadres, assuming that *all* private economic activity was by nature capitalistic, had decided that the scope of domestic sideline occupations should be drastically reduced. This view was denounced in the Party press as "metaphysical"; those officials who had acted severely to restrict sideline occupations were criticized for "lacking any real understanding or concern for the pressing needs of the masses of peasants in their daily life."[20] Individual sideline occupations were officially held to possess a "dual nature": on the one hand, they served a "progressive economic function"; on the other hand, they were "potentially ruinous." To the probable consternation of local officials who had to implement this policy, the dividing line between progress and ruination was thus left indistinct.[21]

Another relatively widespread problem revealed in letters to the

---

[19] *JMJP*, May 21, 1965 (emphasis added).
[20] *JMJP*, October 10, 1965.
[21] See *JMJP*, May 21, 1965; also *Ta Kung Pao* (Peking), March 13, 1965.

major newspapers in the spring and summer of 1965 was the old question of subsidized work-points for basic-level cadres. In the fall of 1964 it had been the official policy that cadres were generally receiving too many subsidized bonuses, and that these should be sharply reduced. In the intervening months, however, the mobilized poor and lower-middle peasants, acting under the supervision of outside work teams, had apparently been overly enthusiastic about cancelling work-points. Not only the excess work-point appropriations of the cadres, but also their *legitimate* allowances, were being forcibly extracted in the form of cash indemnities. In answer to questions by readers, the editors of *Jen-min Jih-pao* declared that "rural basic-level cadres have responsibilities other than labor to fulfill. . . . Commune members should understand that it is fair and reasonable to give basic-level cadres a definite amount of allowance . . . . the cadres should be adequately subsidized."[22]

Another (and related) phenomenon which appeared during the spring and summer of 1965 was a trend toward egalitarianism in the distribution of work-points to the peasants. According to a Yunnan radio broadcast, work-points for peasants were being recorded "rigidly and without reference to how the work is done." Moreover, equal numbers of work-points were assertedly being awarded for performance of unequal tasks, thus leading to a "downward leveling" of individual incomes. Existing income differentials had apparently been interpreted as prima facie evidence of an incipient polarization of classes in the countryside, and the much maligned cadres had thus hastily acted to equalize distribution. In order to discourage this type of thinking and behavior, it was officially stressed that:

> Reasonable work-point levels should be laid down in accordance with the nature and importance of particular jobs; . . . . *it is absolutely impermissible to level down work-points.* . . . The poor and lower-middle peasants should be allowed to give play to their activism, so that they can get reasonable remuneration with steadily increasing incomes.[23]

All of these examples illustrate the confusion resulting from the attempt to establish operational criteria for distinguishing between spontaneous capitalism and legitimate private economic activities, between cadre corruption and proper subsidization, between polarization of classes and peasant activism in production. All can be related directly or indirectly to the ambivalence of Party directives in the first half of 1965 concerning the objects of unity and the objects of struggle in the countryside. It is hardly surprising that a certain amount of confusion should result from this ambivalence. Nor is it surprising that the cadres should become in-

---

22 *JMJP*, May 21, 1965.
23 *Radio Kunming* (Yunnan), April 28, 1965 (emphasis added).

decisive, hesitating to make decisions lest they unknowingly violate imperfectly defined policy guidelines and thus expose themselves to further criticism.

It was not only the basic-level cadres, however, who were confused and indecisive in the spring and summer of 1965; indecision also apparently existed at higher levels. For example, shortly after the First Secretary of the Kwangtung Provincial Party Committee called for a "large-scale mobilization and discussion" among the peasants in order to create a "new socialist countryside" during the interval between spring planting and autumn harvest, a *Jen-min Jih-pao* editorial cautioned that *"we must not launch mass movements in a big way,* hold rallies, or engage in large-scale discussions for everything."[24] Similarly, a speech delivered by T'ao Chu on June 13, in which he gave an extremely optimistic assessment of rural conditions and confidently predicted a "second revolutionary soaring leap" in agricultural production, was rebroadcast two days later containing a freshly inserted passage warning of the serious danger of a capitalist restoration and of the existence of a "number of unsolved problems" which were "unfavorable to the consolidation and development of the collective economy."[25]

---

[24] Compare *NFJP*, March 22, 1965, with *JMJP*, May 10, 1965.

[25] Compare *Radio Canton* (Kwangtung), June 14, 1965, with *Radio Changsha* (Hunan), June 16, 1965.

V
The Turn to Mao-Study

Beginning in July 1965, new efforts were initiated to stimulate an intensive campaign to "study the thought of Mao Tse-tung." This movement was launched, and in the earliest stages received its most emphatic promotion, in the Central-South region. An example of this activity was an "experience-exchange meeting of activists for the study of Chairman Mao's works" held in Canton on August 30, 1965.

While this new campaign to study the thought of Mao claimed a number of broad objectives, it was also intended that it would provide a definitive framework for coping with the unsolved problems in the Socialist Education Movement, and for reducing the normative confusion evident in it during the first half of 1965. The linking of Mao-study to the Socialist Education Movement was repeatedly made explicit. The keynote speaker at the meeting mentioned above emphasized that the study of the thought of Mao was "the most basic guarantee for the success of the Socialist Education Movement."[1]

Directed at cadres and masses alike, the Mao-study movement stressed the need for promoting the spirit of "self reliance" (tzu-li keng-sheng) and "self-sacrifice" (tzu-wo hsi-sheng) among the people. Studying the thought of Mao was to be more than a mere theoretical exercise; it was also the only reliable method for resolving concrete economic and political contradictions—such as those evidenced in the previous six months. For example, in connection with the contradiction between politics and production, it was claimed that "many comrades" had held the view in the past that "good performance in production means good performance in politics." This was criticized on the ground that it failed to answer the key question of whether the production promoted the interests of the collective or the interests of private individuals. By studying Mao's thought, cadres would be able clearly to perceive the priority of collective interests. This would resolve their own ideological problems and at the same time lead to an increase in the masses' enthusiasm for collective production.[2]

Throughout the late summer and fall of 1965, newspaper editorials and Party speeches stressed the need for leading cadres—particularly

---

[1] Speech by Chao Tzu-yang, 1st Secretary of the Kwangtung Provincial Party Committee, reported in *Yang-ch'eng Wan-pao* (Canton) September 8, 1965, and translated in *SCMP* 3540, pp. 1–12.

[2] See the series of articles translated in *CB*, No. 779, January 17, 1966.

43

those at the hsien level and above—to take the lead in studying Mao's thought and personally to guide the movement at the lower levels. In order to ensure that ideology and politics would "take command" in the Mao-study movement, it was announced in the late summer of 1965 that "political instructors" and "political team leaders" would be installed on an experimental basis in production brigades and teams in certain provinces under the direction of regular hsien and commune level Party organizations.[3]

Along with this intensified campaign of Mao-study, a new movement to "revolutionize hsien Party committees" was incorporated into the Socialist Education Movement in October 1965. The *Jen-min Jih-pao* editorial launching this new phase of the campaign summed up the Party's view of the existing situation:

> With the Socialist Education Movement further developed and the socialist consciousness of the broad masses of the peasants universally heightened, building a socialist new countryside has become the most pressing demand of the broad masses. . . . The problem of revolutionizing the leadership of the hsien committee is the key to the revolutionization of rural work as a whole and to building a socialist new countryside.[4]

From mid-October 1965 to March 1966, hsien Party secretaries in all parts of the country underwent "criticism and self-criticism" in order to rid themselves of their "mandarin-like work styles" and their "negative behavior of looking for stability," which assertedly had arisen from "selfishness," "conservatism," "fear of repeating past mistakes," and "lack of courage to make decisions."[5] The remedy for such shortcomings was again proclaimed to be a massive injection of "the thought of Mao Tse-tung." Leading cadres at the hsien level were once more instructed to get out of their offices, go down to the front-lines of production and mingle with the masses "carrying the works of Chairman Mao and implements for labor."[6]

This focusing on the mistakes of leading cadres at the hsien level further diverted attention from the shortcomings of basic-level cadres. The "self-criticism" of a hsien First Secretary in Fukien province is revealing:

> When we meet resistance in carrying out directives from above, we do not seek the reason in the directives themselves, but criticize cadres at the basic levels. We are proud of our "resoluteness" in implementing tasks assigned from above. We listen to opinions only

---

[3] See, for example, *Radio Foochow* (Fukien), August 12, 1965.

[4] *JMJP*, October 12, 1965; also *CB*, No. 779.

[5] For extensive documentation of these assertions and charges, see *China News Analysis* (Hong Kong) No. 605.

[6] *JMJP*, February 8, 1966.

when they conform to our "framework," and we express indignation when they do not. *We always think that the source of all resistance lies in the ideology and understanding of the basic-level cadres and the masses, so we use one-sided reasoning to persuade or even criticize them.* Because we do not listen to differing opinions . . . . we become convinced that the basic-level cadres and the masses agree with us. We were greatly shocked when we read Chairman Mao's teaching that "to carry out directives from upper levels blindly and without reservation is the most subtle way of opposing or sabotaging such directives."[7]

While the Socialist Education Movement thus continued, with emphasis now being given to criticism of leading officials at the hsien level, some new rumblings were being heard on the Chinese political horizon. Beginning with the November 1965 attack against historian-playwright Wu Han, a new campaign of political pressure on intellectuals seemed to be in the offing. At first the nature of this campaign did not seem to differ significantly from the criticism of intellectuals which had occurred in 1964 and 1965.[8] By April 1966, with the initiation of fierce public attacks on leading figures in the Peking Municipal Party Committee, it had become clear, however, that something more fundamental than mere criticism was involved. With the dismissal of Peking Mayor P'eng Chen and the "reorganization" of the Peking Municipal Committee in early June, public notice was given of the birth of the Great Proletarian Cultural Revolution.[9]

When the Central Committee met in plenary session in August 1966, the question was raised as to whether the new revolution should be integrated with the Socialist Education Movement. The thrust of the plenum's decision on this question was that the Socialist Education Movement should, at least temporarily, be insulated from the Cultural Revolution.[10]

This decision was reaffirmed in a number of official statements over the next few months. Chou En-lai, in a speech to a Red Guard rally in Peking on September 15, explicitly instructed the Red Guards *not* to enter industrial plants and rural areas to "exchange revolutionary ex-

---

[7] *JMJP,* October 18, 1965 (emphasis added).

[8] See Adam Oliver, "Rectification of Mainland China Intellectuals, 1964–1965," *Asian Survey,* Vol. V, No. 10 (October, 1965) pp. 475–90.

[9] Reorganization of the Peking Municipal Committee was announced by *NCNA* on June 3. The term "Great Proletarian Cultural Revolution" had been used for the first time by *JMJP* only two days earlier. Prior to that time, the term "great *socialist* cultural revolution" had been used in connection with the attacks on Peking Party personnel and literary figures.

[10] *Decision of the Central Committee of the Chinese Communist Party Concerning the Great Proletarian Cultural Revolution (Adopted August 8, 1966),* Peking: Foreign Languages Press, 1966, Article XIII. In discussing the implementation of the Cultural Revolution, this decision held that where original arrangements for the Socialist Education Movement were appropriate, the Movement should not be interfered with. In some places, however, the Cultural Revolution could be used to "add momentum" to the Socialist Education Movement.

periences." He told the assembled youths that the revolution in these places would proceed according to the original arrangements for the Four Cleans movement.[11]

In December 1966 there was a shift in this policy. The Maoist leadership called for the extension of the Cultural Revolution to the factories and communes in order to "prevent the revolution from stopping halfway."[12] At this point the insulation of the Socialist Education Movement ended, and the Party leadership officially called for the Four Cleans to be channelled into the mainstream of the Cultural Revolution.[13]

[11] *SCMP* No. 3785, September 21, 1966, pp. 3–5.
[12] *JMJP*, December 26, 1966, and January 1, 1967.
[13] *JMJP*, January 1, 1967.

Summary and Conclusions

It is evident, in retrospect, that the Socialist Education Movement passed through five discernible, though not wholly discrete, stages prior to being officially merged with the Cultural Revolution.

The first stage lasted roughly from the Tenth Plenum in September 1962 through the First Ten Points and the summer of 1963. It was marked by general investigations into rural conditions, and by experimentation in socialist education work in a limited number of rural communes. Although sources such as the Lienchiang documents reveal that many problems existed in the Party's rural work in this period, there were no indications that the new campaign would be particularly disruptive, nor that anything other than routine methods of education and indoctrination would be used to correct "erroneous tendencies" in the countryside.

In the second stage, which began with the Later Ten Points of September 1963, the experiments and experiences of the previous year were summarized and concretized into rules and regulations for conduct of the Movement on a nationwide scale. It was during this stage that the Socialist Education Movement first received widespread publicity in the mass media. It was also in this period that peasant associations were organized on a broad scale, work teams dispatched in large numbers to "squat" at the basic levels, rules codified for cadre participation in collective labor, and an attempt made to draw firm class lines in the countryside.

A third stage in the Socialist Education Movement began in September 1964. It involved an operational reorientation of the campaign in accordance with the new pessimistic view of rural conditions as expressed in the Revised Draft of the Later Ten Points. This stage was marked by severe attacks on basic-level cadres for what had previously been regarded as minor errors and deviations. It was also at this time that the call was first issued for a general reclassification of all rural households and for the re-registration of all Party members. In response to a situation officially described as "indeed serious," peasant associations began vigorously to exercise their broad mandate to supervise the cadres, and the restraints on outside work teams relative to the existing basic-level Party and administrative structures were largely removed.

By mid-January 1965 the situation in the countryside had apparently gotten somewhat out of hand, and a fourth stage in the Socialist Education Movement was initiated. Starting with the adoption of the Twenty-three Articles, there was a search for new theoretical guidelines. The apparent objective here was to check indiscriminate attacks against the basic-level cadres, and thus to restore their rapidly declining morale and authority. Although far from unambiguous in its theoretical formulations, the Twenty-three Articles did represent a definite step away from the previous drastic view of the basic-level cadre problem toward a more tolerant view of cadre foibles and shortcomings. Open press and radio criticism of the cadres generally ceased in this period. At the same time, however, obscure references were being made to the existence of an undefined group of "people in positions of authority within the Party who take the capitalist road"—the first known use of a phrase which was to become common during the Cultural Revolution in connection with accusations against Liu Shao-ch'i and other Party leaders under attack.

The fifth stage of the campaign began in the late summer and fall of 1965. A major focus of socialist education work became the rectification of Party officials at the hsien level. They were subjected to intensive "criticism and self-criticism" in order to overcome the prevalent errors of bureaucratism, conservatism, and commandism. The Mao-study movement, and the injunction that politics must "take command" over production, received renewed stress in official Party media. It was also in this period that the first faint tremors of the impending Cultural Revolution were felt in the major cities of China.

It is apparent that certain aspects of the Cultural Revolution bear a family resemblance to ideas and instrumentalities which gained currency during the Socialist Education Movement. It is by no means clear, however, that the two were directly related in any concrete generic or functional sense. The limitations on our present knowledge of this relationship —particularly with respect to the critical "transitional" period from November 1965 to August 1966—still make premature any assumptions about the existence of such a causal nexus.

APPENDIX A*

VIGOROUSLY LAUNCH A LARGE-SCALE PRODUCTION INCREASE, ECONOMY, AND SOCIALIST EDUCATION MOVEMENT†

Ch'en Fu-lung
9 February, 1963

(Record of report to the Hsien Enlarged Three Level Cadre Meeting, draft)

This enlarged meeting today of cadres above the Party branch secretary level throughout the hsien also includes the first secretaries of the commune Party committees, the Party branch secretaries, some commune and brigade leaders, and members of all work teams. The major purpose of the meeting is to study the launching of a large-scale production increase, economy, and socialist education movement.

We recently carried out a socialist education movement, but the effort was insufficient. We are therefore holding a new meeting to study further how such a movement can be broader, more thoroughgoing, and carried out more effectively.

Today, we have three major problems for discussion.

I. *The facts of the previous socialist education movement.*

Our hsien, like other fraternal hsiens, has already carried out a socialist education movement. This has been going on for one month, since the hsien's last enlarged meeting. However, there was a holiday period (the spring festival) so the socialist education movement among the masses lasted only some ten days. During the course of this work, there was a preliminary carrying out of education from the cadres to the masses and from the inside to the outside. Generally speaking, this was done quite well; in some teams, exceptionally well. According to statistics on the entire hsien, 12,247 cadres at the production team level and above were trained, accounting for 93 percent of all the cadres. There were 5,093 Party members who received training, or 94.2 percent of all Party members. In general, 70 to 80 percent of the adult masses were educated. During this period, the commendations for good people and good actions during various types of meetings were combined. There were 3,621 people commended as good cadres, 1,053 commended as good Party members, 742 commended as good Youth League members, and 5,644 commended as good commune members, with the result that there was an increase of good styles and a decrease of bad. Consequently, we consider all of the work for this period as good, and the launching of the campaign as normal and healthy.

Our major achievements were the following.

1) A majority of the cadres heightened their socialist awareness by means of this education. It was made clear that being a cadre was for the purpose of serving the people, and many of the cadres became firmer in their revolutionary resolve. Many cadres changed their past thinking about not wanting to be cadres. The saying had been common: "We won't do it, get someone else." But as a result, work was undertaken with great resolve. According to statistics, before the campaign, there were 172 brigade cadres and 1,016 production team cadres who said they did not want to be cadres and asked for

* Translated from *Fu-chien Lien-chiang Hsien fei-fang wen-chien chi ch'i yen-hsi* (Documents of the Bandit Authorities of Lienchiang Hsien, Fukien, and Their Analysis) (Taipei: Kai-tsao Ch'u-pan-she, July 1964), pp. 41–51.

† *Chin-i-pu k'ai-chan i-ko ta-kuei-mo-ti tseng-ch'an chieh-yüeh, she-hui chu-i chiao-yü yün-tung.*

a change of jobs. Most of these changed their minds as a result of the education campaign and now there are very few who do not want to be cadres. According to a report at the meeting, there were only four of these people at the level of the brigade, and 163 at the level of the production team. According to the statistics of the Ao-chiang Commune, 195 cadres originally did not want to be cadres; now there are only ten. This is a very great achievement.

2) The knowledge of the broad mass of commune members (including cadres) began to rise and directions became clear. They recognized that such methods as "contracting production to the households," doing things on one's own, and having one's own land, agricultural implements, and fishing gear were incorrect. It was recognized that the crux of these practices was the problem of the struggle between the two roads, and the reflection of the class struggle. As a result, a majority of the cadres took the land originally contracted to the households, agricultural implements, and fishing gear and turned them over to the production teams, thus returning them to collective ownership. According to statistics, 755 production teams, 96.3 percent of the total number of teams, recovered land that had been "contracted for production to the households." The area of the land returned was 4,218 mou, or 97 percent of the land "contracted to the households for production." In addition, 5,722, or 70 percent, of the agricultural implements that had been turned over to the households were recovered, as well as 121 boats and 43 nets. This is very good.

3) Bad habits decreased and good ones began to increase. The enthusiasm of the broad mass of commune members for collective production has gone up. For example, at present the number of people who have given up agriculture and gone into business to speculate has decreased greatly, and a majority of those who went away have now returned. Those who did not originally participate in collective production are now doing so. The condition of individual commune members haphazardly reclaiming fields on the whole no longer exists, and the uncontrolled cutting of forests has been stopped. Feudal superstition has also decreased, even to the point where some of the cadres and masses have taken it upon themselves to smash idols, a situation quite evident in coastal areas. In the past, these people were enthusiastic about repairing Buddhist temples and engaging in superstitious practices. Now they show no great enthusiasm for this, while some have done away with temples and converted them into granaries. Extravagant spending during the spring festival and gambling (especially the latter) have decreased greatly from last year. As a result, social order is being well maintained.

4) Some of the backward teams or teams in difficulty also began to change for the better during the course of this drive. Eighty-six production brigades throughout the hsien are presently carrying out production very effectively. Of these, 21 brigades had been basically backward in production, but are now producing well. Some have already caught up with teams that were originally advanced producers. The Ao-chiang commune originally had 98 backward production teams. At present, 61, or 62 percent, have changed. The Wang-ya Brigade of the Tanyang commune had been rather backward in production all along. During the course of this work, production picked up and is now being carried out very effectively. Even in comparison with other teams in the commune, this brigade can be considered a relatively good one. Other localities have similar conditions. Kuei-an and Chu-pu along the P'an-tu [River] had 12 production teams that were relatively backward or in great difficulties. A majority of them improved during the course of this work, with some of them overtaking other teams with relatively good production and

outdoing them several fold. They outdid them in tilling, burning stubble off the fields, dredging mud from rivers, and accumulating fertilizer.

Generally speaking, the ideological awareness of the broad cadres and masses has been further raised, an enthusiastic tide for production has taken form, and bad habits have decreased while good ones have increased. These are overall accomplishments, but we must still look at the problems. Our work is insufficient, especially in xxxx [x's in original]. If we look at our work in the spirit of this meeting, it is still insufficient and many problems exist. What are these problems? The major ones are:

1) Although we put great effort into conducting the campaign, the scope of its influence is still not great. This is especially the case with the large-scale mass drive which has not yet taken shape. We are still fighting for time and going through the process, and ideological problems have not been resolved thoroughly and clearly. Some places are even more remiss and some people have not even met the demands of the hsien.

2) Looking at the matter from the whole hsien, the condition is good and accomplishments are great. However, things are unbalanced: what is good is very good and what is bad is very bad. Some teams have not even held meetings; they did not even hold meetings of cadres or Youth League members. Out of a hundred people, only several dozen showed up, and in some teams, only 40 or 50 percent of the members were educated.

3) The contents of socialist education were not put forth in an overall manner, but rather monotonously; as a result, problems were not solved thoroughly. Everyone knows that the contents of education consisted of situation education, class education, and policy education, but this is not enough. Feudalism and the squandering of money basically were not mentioned. As a result, bad practices have not been crushed! We are still not handling well enough such problems as speculation, superstitious practices, religious festivals and money marriage (not in general, but where this has become a trafficking in people).

Why do these problems still exist? For which reasons? At this two-day meeting of the Enlarged Hsien Standing Committee, we unanimously recognize that the most basic cause of this problem in production has been our failure to recognize sufficiently the great importance of the socialist education movement. We have failed to understand deeply where the significance of socialist education lies. Consequently, our determination and organization of forces have not been great enough and our study of problems has been insufficient. This is to say, the important and most basic cause has been our failure to recognize sufficiently the significance of the socialist education campaign, the most important problem that we have. Our hsien committee must review this point and not be angry with the people, the commune, team cadres, or work teams.

II. *Recognize further the significance of socialist education.*

Why do we want to launch a large-scale production increase, economy, and socialist education campaign? Everyone knows that our overall conditions here in Lienchiang, like the conditions throughout the country and the province, are good and better from year to year. However, we must strive for even better conditions in 1963 and thereafter. What is the most important task that we have at present? Basically, and speaking in terms of work, it is how to obtain a bumper harvest in 1963. At present, the aims of all our work are directed to this, which means not only a bumper harvest in grains, but in all crops, and an overall increase in production. At a recent Provincial Party Congress, Chairman Mao said, "Close ranks, fight energetically, overcome difficulties, achieve victory." These four phrases constitute the aims of our work. Our situation has improved from year to year, but not enough. There are still difficulties. The problem of grains has been solved, but we still have the problem of things for wear and use. So Chairman Mao has said that we must close ranks, fight energetically, overcome difficulties, and achieve victory. We must also realize an overall increase in output and a bumper crop for 1963 and, in line with the directions of Chairman Mao, we must mobilize all Party members, Youth League members, cadres, and active elements so that together they can lead the masses in undertaking all types of production effectively. However, effective production primarily depends on people and on their enthusiasm, sense of awareness, and initiative. It cannot be achieved without these things. Production must be carried out by the people and by the masses, and there must be leadership by the Party and cadres. However, if cadres mobilize people without a sufficiently high sense of awareness, production will not be effective. To achieve this aim, we must, in line with the arrangements made by the provincial Party committee, launch a large-scale production increase, economy, and socialist education drive. At present, this is the most important, the most pressing, and most demanding task. We know that we are only one month and a half away from the busy spring planting season. Chairman Mao has said of this period of the year that "the opportunity must not be lost, it will not come again." We are now in this great period of time. Organizations at all levels above the Party branch and all the cadres must pay attention to this opportune time, make a great resolve, and concentrate the greatest effort to undertake this campaign effectively. This also means that, going on from the advanced base of the last campaign, the socialist education movement must be undertaken more gloriously and on a larger scale and that the work must be carried out deeper and more thoroughly. This is what is demanded of us. Why do we say that this campaign is the most important, pressing, and urgent task of the present time? The reasons for this are:

1) We all know that for effective production and progress in all areas of work, failure to solve the basic ideological problems will mean ineffective results. Chairman Mao has said that to look at things and not at people is to do an ineffective job. "To look at things and not at people" means to pay attention only to specific things and to disregard the ideological work of people. There is a lot of work at present. This means production in agriculture, forestry, pastoral industry, subsidiary industry, and fishing. There are many phases of this work. Nevertheless, the most important thing is still to pay attention to ideological work and to the socialist education campaign. Without this, things cannot be done well. It is quite obvious to everyone that in the mere span of one month (actually, only some 10 days of work among the masses), great changes were made in the rural situation, as well as in the social, production, and the spiritual conditions of the people. If we do this even more thoroughly, the changes effected will certainly be even better. When we engage in production, we do battle with the world of nature, fighting just as the People's Liberation Army does. The PLA can fight victoriously. It drove out US imperialism and annihilated the 8-million man army of the Kuomintang. Recently the PLA achieved a great victory on the Sino-Indian border, annihilating and capturing several thousand of the enemy. Why was this possible? It was because of ideological work! It was political work! Our officers and men were able to carry on with the temperature at more than 30 degrees below zero, on high mountains where the air is thin and it was difficult to breathe, where everything was snow and ice, and where one's ears

and nose froze. The Indian troops were not able to do this. As soon as they were engaged, they surrendered! It is therefore perfectly clear that we must not look at things and disregard people, that we cannot pay attention only to specific conditions and disregard ideological work. Everyone also knows that during the 10 years following liberation the general line was promulgated in 1953 and that a great effort was made in education. There was a similar effort in 1958, and there have also been such things as education for cooperativization. These things having been done well, conditions were very good. In recent years, we encountered difficulties and some shortcomings in our work. During the course of summarizing experiences and lessons and while improving shortcomings and mistakes in work, we slackened in our socialist education for cadres and for the masses. Now capitalist and feudalist thinking has again reared its head among some people. If we fail to take a firm grasp of ideological work and only concern ourselves with specific work and pay attention only to production, it will not do.

2) The socialist education movement at present is not merely for the sake of present production, but for production and work in the future. If we see the matter as a great effort in production and as a bumper crop only for this year, that is too simple. Unless we lay an ideological foundation for the next several years, the next several decades, even the next 100 years, it will not do. If we do not do this, then our work will be like trying to cure a headache by treating the head. You pay attention to wherever there are problems, but not to what is important and what is basic.

You ask about bad customs. Is it all right not to oppose them and do nothing? It is not. While you engage in production, these people engage in speculation, practice Buddhism, and hold religious ceremonies. At present, money marriages, trafficking in people, religious fraud, and gambling all exist. In the Hua-wu Brigade of Ao-chiang, there were 18 girls. Their average age was 14 and the average price was 750 yuan. In Pai-sha there was a girl who was married 13 times. Some people sell women like hogs. They weigh and sell them by the *chin*. Even worse are some people who do a business in women. What kind of behavior is trafficking in people! They hold out their hand and introduce you to someone for 50 yuan. They hold out their hand again and its another 50 yuan. These people do not work but engage in business for speculation. In some places, waste and spending is rampant. Public accumulation is also wasted, even to the point where the distribution made to the commune members is all used up. It is quite obvious that if the commune members do not have money their production will be in great difficulty and they will have to ask the state for loans. How can this kind of behavior be all right? We have to make a great effort in opposing it.

As everyone knows, we are at present opposing revisionism and we are fighting it internationally. China is a socialist country and the masses of people are the masters. If we do not do well the things that we mentioned, will we become a capitalist country? There are facts with regard to this. Everyone knows that originally Yugoslavia was a socialist country; now capitalism has been restored, land can be bought and sold freely, there are a great number of rich peasants, and more than 90 percent of the land is worked individually. We have to think about China and we have to think of ways to prevent it from becoming like that. Everyone knows that if these bad practices, capitalism, and feudalist thinking and behavior are not taken care of and oppressed, or particularly if we allow them to develop further, capitalism could be restored and the problem would become grave. Therefore, in undertaking this campaign not only must production and other work be performed effectively, but this campaign must be our plan for 100 years. We must ensure that China will always be a socialist country. Let everyone take stock to see whether or not it will do not to carry out the campaign effectively. The condition in the world today is that the East wind is prevailing over the West wind, but in some places this is not the case. It is the West wind prevailing over the East wind. For this reason, we must resolve to carry out the campaign effectively.

We want to carry out such a campaign, but do we want to carry out a large campaign? We do. It must be done with an allout effort and with great force. It cannot be carried out in an ordinary way. The masses must be mobilized boldly. We have to see clearly that if the campaign is not undertaken on a large scale, we will not be able to crush who knows which types of bad practices, capitalism, and feudalism and to heighten the awareness of cadres and the masses. Achievements were scored the last time we carried out such a campaign, but are all these achievements secure? Some people carrying on by themselves and engaging in speculation are still lying low. They are waiting for the movement to be over so that they can again take up their practices. Some bad people are creating rumors, taking the lead, and fanning dissension. Others with a low level of ideological awareness will then again be able to get together with them and "contract production down to the households," carry on individually, and engage in speculation. These things exist. It is for this reason that we must make a great effort. We cannot go about it in an ordinary way, but we must do it in the same manner that we did things during 1953 when the general line was promulgated and during 1958 when the great leap forward was going on.

Is it necessary to struggle? This is a great problem. Struggle is still needed. If you do not fight, then others will force you to fight. We must combat capitalism, feudalism, and the political degenerates, but when we say struggle, we refer to ideological struggle as the most important. This means using all forms and methods of fighting. Naturally, some people will have to be dealt with according to the law, while others will have to be handled differently. This is also the way it should be within the Party, the Youth League, and among the cadres and the rank and file. The extremely bad elements should be dealt with according to the law, but this will involve only extreme cases whose number will be very small. The others should be handled by ideological struggle, but ideological struggle should also be applied to those who have to be dealt with according to the law. If we examine the carrying out of this great movement in terms of the thinking of a small number of comrades, will it be possible for problems to crop up and for things to be done wrong? If there are mistakes it will mean that we Party branch secretaries, brigade leaders, commune chiefs, secretaries, and work teams did not do things effectively. Later we will have to criticize ourselves, make reviews, and place the blame, even to the extent of making restitution, apologizing, and pacifying others. This is a possibility, but we must not worry about it. The campaign must be undertaken, the struggle must be launched. As everyone knows, in the last two years we proposed that work should be done thoroughly, but this is not equivalent to undertaking the campaign. The campaign must still be undertaken. If the campaign is carried out correctly, there is no need to worry; if we make only a half-hearted effort, we now see that it will not do. At present, a small number of people still engage in speculation, traffic in people, and depend upon superstition for a living.

Why must there be struggle? This struggle has existed from the beginning. Classes still exist, and as long as there are classes there is a class struggle.

These things exist objectively. If you do not fight, then others will "contract production to the households," engage in speculation, and traffic in people. Do you still ask whether we should make an effort and whether we should struggle? There is one important thing which we should understand. That is, whether we recognize it or not, classes exist and there is a class struggle. To fear the class struggle and not engage in it resolutely, to coexist peacefully, to have a peaceful transition, and not to fight, these things constitute revisionism. This is the reason that people are afraid of going too far. If there are problems and things are done incorrectly, they must be checked and corrected. It does no good to worry about them. The struggle we are now engaging in is not the same as that of the past. We now have experiences and can do things better. Problems cannot arise if we study conscientiously, act in compliance with stipulations, not put forward our own assertions, follow the Party's policies, do things according to the rules, and pay attention to work methods.

It is well known that the level of our cadres, including our comrades at the hsien level, is not very high at present. We still do not understand sufficiently the experiences of struggle. For example, we still cannot distinguish two different contradictions. We still do not fully understand the complexity of the class struggle, because this struggle occurs in politics, the military, in economics, culture, with and without form, in open and in hidden forms, and inside the Party and outside, which makes it very complicated. In addition, we still do not understand too well the differences in the class struggle during the period of socialism and during the period of the democratic revolution, nor are we too clear about the differences in the class struggle after and before seizing power. We are also not too clear about art in the class struggle during the period of socialist construction. However, we should not worry about this, for if we do not understand we will study and we will do things conscientiously according to the stipulations of the Party. If we decide to study during the course of work, then we will be able to carry out the campaign effectively.

III. *The contents of socialist education.*

The original setting forth of the contents of socialist education now does not look wholly complete, and we must again restudy this matter in line with the desires of the provincial Party committee. Premier Chou En-lai made a good speech at the Meeting of All Advanced Collective Representatives of East China convened in Shanghai by the East China Area. He discussed eight problems, and the East China Bureau has decided to make these the program for carrying out socialist education in the villages and cities of that area. The themes of these eight problems were:

1) The collective first, the individual second; the problem of ownership and agricultural production.

2) The state first, the individual second; the problem of production and work.

3) Make demands on oneself first, then on others. This is also the problem of production and work.

4) One's own responsibility first, that of others second; the problem of the mutual relationship among people in labor and in work.

5) First take care of public property, then of private property: the problem of distribution.

6) For the public first, for oneself second: the problem in politics and ideology.

7) One for the benefit of all the people, all the people for the benefit of

one. All the people here refers to all the laboring people who are building the socialist road under the leadership of the working class.

8) We for the whole world, the whole world for us: primarily emphasizing the problem of internationalism.

The present provincial Party committee has proposed the Three Three's and made them the contents for carrying our socialist education throughout the province:

The First Three is propagating the three "isms," that is, collectivism, patriotism, and socialism.

The Second Three is opposing three bad styles, that is, the capitalist style, the feudalist style, and the style of extravagance and waste.

The Third Three is supporting resolutely the three must's, that is, we must resolutely go the road of socialism, we must be concerned about loving and protecting the collective, and we must operate the commune democratically and frugally (which includes teaching the commune members to run their own households frugally).

We should now like to make clear why these things have to be done and why the Three Three's were put forth, especially why everyone must oppose the three evil styles. Everyone should be aware that the great advantage of this is that our program is quite clear, and that there is no question about what we must do and what we must support. By setting things forth this way, the masses are also clear about what must be opposed, supported, and what must and must not be done. If we did otherwise, the program for our movement would not be in detail and this would make it weak and incomplete. By doing it this way, it is easy to understand and remember, and things can be done effectively because the program is clear. After the program is thus clarified, the differences between right and wrong, and between good and bad, are differentiated very clearly and there can be no confusion. At the same time, once the program is clear, the campaign will have force and possess rich contents. In addition, it is clear whether or not it is right not to oppose the feudalist style and the style of extravagance. It is not right not to oppose them. The key point in the previous phase of our work was situation education and class education. This was good and the achievements were very great. Our efforts in the struggle between the two roads is also notable, but it was not done effectively enough with regard to the styles of feudalism and extravagance. In the previous effort, there was a basic failure on our part to oppose such things as money marriages, trafficking in people, and using women for gain. Viewing the situation at the moment, it seems that the efforts in situation education, the struggle between the two roads, and class education are even better; but it will not do if these problems are not taken care of. If there is no opposition to the feudalist style, then it will be very difficult to consolidate and develop the collective economy, a point which was not made clear in the past. Now it is quite clear. In the past we consistently opposed "contracting production to the household," but you now know about money marriages. A woman will be given in marriage of 800, 1,000 or 2,000 yuan. Some people now say: engaging in speculation was for no other reason than that XXX wanted a wife. If things are done in this way, labor efforts will be dissipated and no one will look after the collective.

Will it do not to attack speculation? It will not. Lenin said:

> The proletariat which has overcome the bourgeoisie must continue to implement the basic policy line regarding peasants thoroughly and consistently. That is, the proletariat must separate the working peasants from

those who do not, which means, on one hand, peasants who work, XX [characters missing in text], and plant land and, on the other hand, peasants who engage in speculation. This division is fully within the essence of socialism. It was the laboring peasants who helped the starving workers in the city by turning over 100 million *pood* of foodstuffs to the state organs at government-fixed prices, even though at that time these organs had many shortcomings. (The workers' state recognized the shortcomings clearly, but there was no way to avoid them during the period of the transition to socialism.) These working peasants are the full and worthy comrades of the socialist workers, the most dependable allies of the socialist workers, and their brothers in the struggle to oppose capitalist oppression. As to the other type of peasants, they cheated the state, made all-out efforts to undertake XX [characters missing in text] in various localities, engaged in arson and robbery, speculated, took advantage of the hunger and difficulties of workers in the cities, secretly used prices 10 times greater than those set by the state, and sold more than 40 million *pood* of foodstuffs—these peasants were traitors to commerce, the allies of the capitalists, the class enemies of the workers, and exploiters.

Consequently, speculation, trafficking in people, religious frauds, and gambling are the objects of our opposition to the feudalist and capitalist styles. They are the objects of our attack.

Waste and extravagance must also be opposed for they are the opposite of running communes economically and frugally. At present, production and livelihood are still not very good and there are difficulties; but some people, even including some cadres, want to build attractive meeting places and houses and spend large amounts of money derived from the distribution of income and from public accumulation on these projects. Some call on the masses to engage in obligatory work to cut down collective trees, and use bricks that belong to the collective for building. These people know better. If they are not opposed, it will be difficult to consolidate and develop the people's communes and the collective economy. It is for this reason that the provincial committee has proposed the Three Three's as the educational content of this campaign for the reasons given here.

If we cadres at all levels do anything that is not good during this phase, we should check it and carry out criticism and self-criticism. Individuals in serious violation of the law or discipline should be dealt with. The masses expect a lot of us during this period. For example, if a small number of cadres are not correct or not fully correct in building houses, the masses will take a dim view of this. They will say, "The monthly wages of one of our cadres are only 20 or 30 yuan. How can he build such a house, and such a big one!" These would be natural doubts for the masses. However, we have already talked about the problem of cadres building houses. They should be built where there is justification, and assistance should also be provided when it is necessary and possible. However, some people are not correct or not fully correct. Some use money meant for public accumulation or from distribution accounts of commune members, others cut down collective forests, while still others appropriate the funds and bricks, even the labor and land, of the brigade. This is extremely vicious. There are also some who build houses for themselves and get the commune members to contribute money. This is even more mistaken. All these things belong to the category of evil practices and must now be done away with. If they are not, the masses will say that socialist education only educates the masses, not the cadres. What would this mean? It could only mean that the serious and outstanding problems of our cadres had not been resolved and that the masses had taken a dim view of this.

APPENDIX B* (THE FIRST TEN POINTS)

DRAFT RESOLUTION OF THE CENTRAL COMMITTEE OF THE CHINESE COMMUNIST PARTY ON SOME PROBLEMS IN CURRENT RURAL WORK †

May 20, 1963

The Central Committee has adopted resolutions or issued directives for solution of some of the problems existing in current rural work. But there are still other problems that have yet to be solved. Of these, some were merely pointed out in directives in the past. But as they were not presented in a clear-cut and systematic way, they have not received the due attention of the people. It is therefore necessary that these problems be explained again in a manner that is both clear and systematic.

There are altogether ten such problems, all inter-related. It has taken us 13 years of practice since the establishment of our government to produce a relatively complete document on the problems in rural work. Especially in the past three years—from 1960, when the Central Committee promulgated the 12 items of work for reorganization of rural society, to the present—we have worked hard to draft this resolution. It is obvious therefore, that in the course of acquainting oneself with objective matters, the process of repetitive practice is essential.

Where do correct ideas come from? Do they drop from the skies? No. Are they innate in the mind? No. They come from social practice, and from it alone; they come from three kinds of social practice—the struggle for production, the class struggle and scientific experiment. It is man's social being that determines his thinking. Once the correct ideas characteristic of the advanced class are grasped by the masses, these ideas turn into a material force which changes society and changes the world. In their social practice, men engage in various kinds of struggle and gain rich experience, both from their successes and from their failures. Countless phenomena of the objective external world are reflected in a man's brain through his five sense organs—the organs of sight, hearing, smell, taste and touch. At first, knowledge is perceptual. The leap to conceptual knowledge, *i.e.*, to ideas, occurs when sufficient perceptual knowledge is accumulated. This is one process in cognition. It is the first stage in the whole process of cognition, the stage leading from objective matter to subjective consciousness, from existence to ideas. Whether or not one's consciousness or ideas (including theories, policies, plans or measures) do correctly reflect the laws of the objective external world is not yet proved at this stage, in which it is not yet possible to ascertain whether they are correct or not. Then comes the second stage in the process of cognition, the stage leading from consciousness back to matter, from ideas back to existence, in which the knowledge gained in the first stage is applied in social practice to ascertain whether the theories, policies, plans or measures meet with the anticipated success. Generally speaking, those that succeed are correct and those that fail are incorrect, and this is especially true of man's struggle with nature. In

* Acknowledgment is made of a translation in *Issues & Studies,* Institute of International Relations, Taipei, Vol. II, No. 8 (May 1966) pp. 46–60. This translation has been checked against the Chinese text and some editorial revisions made by the authors and the staff of the Center for Chinese Studies.

† *Chung-kung chung-yang kuan-yü mu-ch'ien nung-ts'un kung-tso chung jo-kan wen-t'i ti chüeh-ting (ts'ao-an).*

social struggle, the forces representing the advanced class sometimes suffer defeat not because their ideas are incorrect but because, in the balance of forces engaged in struggle, they are not as powerful for the time being as the forces of reaction; they are therefore temporarily defeated, but they are bound to triumph sooner or later. Man's knowledge makes another leap through the test of practice. This leap is more important than the previous one. For it is this leap alone that can prove the correctness or incorrectness of the first leap, *i.e.*, of the ideas, theories, policies, plans or measures formulated in the course of reflecting the objective external world. There is no other way of testing truth. Furthermore, the one and only purpose of the proletariat in knowing the world is to change it. Often, a correct idea can be arrived at only after many repetitions of the process leading from matter to consciousness and then back to matter, that is, leading from practice to knowledge and then back to practice. Such is the Marxist theory of knowledge, the dialectical materialist theory of knowledge. Among our comrades there are many who do not yet understand this theory of knowledge. When asked the source of their ideas, opinions, policies, methods, plans and conclusions, eloquent speeches and long articles, they consider the question strange and cannot answer it. Nor do they comprehend that matter can be transformed into consciousness and consciousness into matter, although such leaps are phenomena of everyday life. It is therefore necessary to educate our comrades in the dialectical materialist theory of knowledge, so that they can orientate their thinking correctly, become good at investigation and study and at summing up experience, overcome difficulties, commit fewer mistakes, do their work better, and struggle hard so as to build China into a great and powerful socialist country and help the broad masses of the oppressed and exploited throughout the world in fulfilment of our great internationalist duty.

Attached to this resolution are the following reference materials: Two reports from the Party committees of Hunan and Hopei provinces; one report from Comrade Sung Jen-ch'iung of the Northeast Bureau; one report from the Party committee of Honan province; two reports from the Party committee of Hunan province; four reports from hsien, region, and commune committees of Honan, Hupeh, and Hunan; one set of data re-issued from Hsiyang hsien of Shansi province; and two sets of data from Chekiang province, totalling twenty items. Although numerous, these materials are good reading despite their bulk. It is best to read them before perusing the rest of the resolution, because these data are of great importance and are well written. Basically, this resolution was written on the basis of these data. Without these data, the drawing of such a systematic resolution would have been impossible.

What exactly are the ten problems of current rural work? They are:

I. THE SITUATIONAL PROBLEM

After the Central Committee set forth in 1961 the 60 Articles governing rural work, it again issued the directive on the sending down of basic accounting units to the countryside and on readjustment of rural burdens. Except for areas seriously stricken by natural calamities and those ill-managed communes and brigades, the situation in the entire rural area has improved greatly, and agricultural production has increased gradually. In September, 1962, the Central Committee promulgated a resolution on the strengthening of the collective economy of the people's communes and the development of agricultural production. It also issued a revised draft of the 60 Articles, which had enormous impact on the further strengthening of the collective economy and on developing agricultural production. Today agricultural production has hit new highs in many places. Conditions of agricultural production in the whole country are becoming better each year. The development of agricultural production is producing great impact on accelerating the development of the national economy. All this serves to explain that it was groundless for some comrades to entertain pessimistic views in the past towards the rural situation and the conditions of agricultural production. All this also proves the total correctness and greatness of the Party in raising high the Three Red Banners of the General Line, the People's Communes, and the Great Leap Forward.

II. The Problem of Whether Class, Class Contradiction, and Class Struggle Still Exist in a Socialist Society

At the Central Committee's working conference at Peitaiho in August, 1962, and at the 10th plenum of the 8th Central Committee in September of the same year, Comrade Mao Tse-tung repeatedly pointed out that the socialist society is a relatively long historical stage; that in this stage there still exist class, class contradiction, and class struggle; and that also existent is the struggle between socialism and capitalism and the danger of a comeback of capitalism. He emphasized that this kind of struggle would be a long and complex one. He also pointed out that correct understanding and handling of class contradiction and class struggle, and correct handling of the contradiction between ourselves and the enemy and also the internal contradictions of the people, are essential in leading and uniting the people in order to carry out smoothly socialist reforms and socialist construction. The resolution adopted by the Party's Central Committee in regard to its rural work policy was based on this thought of Comrade Mao Tse-tung. His analysis and logical reasoning of the problem of classes and their contradictions in socialism have greatly enriched and expanded Marxism and Leninism. Any departure from this correct analysis and logical reasoning will inevitably cause our work of socialist construction to lose its direction, thus making it impossible for our agriculture to develop healthily along the road of socialism.

The communique of the tenth plenum of the 8th Central Committee, which has great and important historical significance, said:

> Throughout the historical period of proletarian revolution and proletarian dictatorship, throughout the historical period of transition from capitalism to communism — which will last for scores of years or even longer—there is class struggle between the proletariat and the bourgeoisie and struggle between socialism and capitalism. The reactionary ruling classes which have been overthrown are not reconciled to their doom. They always attempt to stage a comeback.
>
> Meanwhile, there still exist in society bourgeois influences, the force of habit of the old society, and a spontaneous tendency toward capitalism among part of the small producers. Therefore, among the people a small number of persons making up only a tiny fraction of the total population who have not yet undergone socialist remolding always attempt to depart from the socialist road and turn to the capitalist road whenever there is an opportunity. Class struggle is inevitable under these circumstances.

III. The Present Emergence of Severe and Sharp Class Struggle in Chinese Society

Many facts brought to light concerning today's society prove the correctness of this assertion on class struggle.

1) The exploiting class, landlords and rich peasants who have been over-

thrown are always trying to stage a comeback. They are waiting for an opportunity to counterattack in order to carry out class revenge, and to deal a blow against the poor peasants and lower-middle peasants.

2) Landlords and rich peasants who have been overthrown are employing all kinds of schemes in an attempt to corrupt our cadres in order to usurp the leadership and power. In some communes and brigades the leadership and power actually have fallen into their hands. In some sectors of other organizations they also have their agents.

3) In some places landlords and rich peasants are carrying out activities for the restoration of feudalistic patriarchal rule, putting out counter-revolutionary propaganda, and developing counter-revolutionary organizations.

4) Landlords, rich peasants, and counter-revolutionaries are making use of religion and the reactionary *hui-tao-men* [secret, religious, and welfare societies] to deceive the masses and carry out criminal activities.

5) Various sabotage activities of the reactionaries, such as sabotage of public properties, collection of intelligence, or even murder and arson, have been discovered in many places.

6) In commerce, the activities of speculation and profiteering have reached serious proportions. In some places, such activities are rampant.

7) The phenomena of exploiting hired hands, high-interest loans, buying and selling of land have also occurred.

8) In addition to the old bourgeoisie who continue to engage in speculation and profiteering activities, there also emerge in today's society new bourgeois elements who have become rich by speculation.

9) In organizations and the collective economy, there have emerged a group of corrupt elements, thieves, speculators, and degenerates who have ganged up with landlords and rich peasants to commit evil deeds. These elements are a part of the new bourgeoisie, or their ally.

These facts have combined to give us a most serious lesson: Never at any moment should we forget the class struggle, forget the proletarian dictatorship, forget to rely on the poor and the lower-middle peasants, forget the Party policies, forget the Party work.

IV. The Question of Whether Our Comrades Have Clearly Seen the Seriousness of This Hostile Situation

It should be stated that not all our comrades have paid attention to the various kinds of class struggle phenomena mentioned above. Many have not observed these phenomena and given them the serious thought required. Instead, they adopt an attitude of indifference, thereby letting the phenomena continue and develop. The February 8, 1963, report from the Hunan provincial committee, which Comrade Mao Tse-tung endorsed and relayed to the Central Committee, has correctly reflected the problem. The report says: "Some comrades have put it well in saying 'How can we achieve socialist construction when there is peaceful co-existence in politics, the attitude of muddling in organization, and the attitude of superficialty in economics?' " For this reason, the Central Committee believes that among our cadres and Party members, efforts should be made through socialist education to rectify the standpoint of the proletariat, overcome the mistakes that cause betrayal of the proletarian standpoint, so that our cadres and Party members can correctly provide the leadership for the great majority of the masses in carrying on class struggle and the struggle between socialism and capitalism. Upon this hinges the fundamental issue that determines the success or failure of our socialist enterprise.

61

V. The Question of Whom to Rely Upon

Either in revolution or in socialist construction, the question of who are to be relied upon and who are to be won over must be settled. The proletariat and its vanguards must rely upon real and dependable forces in order to be able to win over prospective allies, and to isolate the enemy of the proletariat and the people. When carrying out land reform and overthrowing the land-lord class, and when agricultural collectivization and socialist reforms are being implemented, the Party's class line in the rural areas is to rely upon poor peasants and lower-middle peasants, and to unite with the middle peasants. But how about this class line after agricultural collectivization is realized? Would it be changed? It is said that some people are of the conviction that "since all products will be public property after the realization of the cooperative system, and everybody without exception will be earning their meals against their work points, there will be no need for division of classes and the class line." There are also others who believe that "agrarian reform should rely upon the poor peasants, production should rely on the middle peasants." People who have such a viewpoint are unaware of the class sentiment of the proletariat, and without understanding of class viewpoint and of reality. In fact, they also fail to understand the basic viewpoint of the masses.

At the time of land reform and collectivization, the poor peasants (including the old hired hands) and the lower-middle peasants constituted the bulk of the farming population. They were the proletariat and the semi-proletariat of the rural areas. They were the opponents of the exploitation system and the exploiting class. They were the most active supporters of the socialist line and collective economy. Reliance on the poor and the lower-middle peasants should be the long-range class line of the Party. In the whole historical stage of socialism, and before the stage of communism is reached, if we, in carrying out socialist reforms and socialist construction in the rural areas, and in developing agricultural production, do not rely on them, who else then is there to rely upon? If we do not rely on them, how shall we be able effectively to strengthen our unity with the middle peasants? They are the social foundation on which we can build up socialist and communist enterprises in rural areas.

In rural areas, the proletarian dictatorship can be realized only by relying upon the poor peasants and the lower-middle peasants. They are the only ones to rely upon for the formation of a strong alliance of workers and peasants, for the expert management of the nation, for achieving a good collective economy, for the effective suppression and remolding of all the hostile elements, and for smashing the encirclement formed by the spontaneous capitalistic forces. Otherwise, all these would be impossible to attain. Hence, comrades in Hunan have this to say: "To separate from the poor peasants and the lower-middle peasants is tantamount to losing the left and right hands. It will be like a commander without troops, whose words fall on deaf ears, and who is without help in doing anything and unable to move even an inch." This statement hits the nail on the head.

VI. The Problem Regarding the Correct Method and Policy for Carrying Out the Socialist Education Movement in Rural Areas at Present

Basing itself on Comrade Mao Tse-tung's directives issued at the Peitaiho conference in August 1962 in relation to class, situation, and contradiction, the Central Committee considers a socialist education movement must be universally carried out in rural areas in order to demarcate the contradictions between ourselves and the enemy, and the internal contradictions of the people. It is also to distinguish right from wrong, thereby rallying together more than 95 percent of the peasant masses and the rural cadres to jointly deal with the enemy of socialism, to continue with the thorough execution of the revised draft of the 60 Articles on sending down the basic accounting units to the countryside, all for the development of agricultural production. The method of education lies in teaching the cadres and masses the directives of Comrade Mao Tse-tung, the Central Committee resolutions on the strengthening of collective economy and on agricultural production, the revised draft of the 60 Articles, and this current resolution of the Central Committee. Such lectures should also cover the specific situation, concrete cases, and work of that locality, so as to bring out the initiative of local cadres and people. This can be done by carrying on discussions and asking questions at the same time. The local cadres and the masses will be enabled to grasp the thinking of the Central Committee and Comrade Mao Tse-tung, to understand the correct method of handling the contradictions between ourselves and the enemy as well as the internal contradictions of the people. They will be enabled to learn the working methods of taking the mass line. At the same time, those cadres who have committed mistakes of various degrees of seriousness and frequency can wash their hands and bodies and shed their burdens, so that they may come face to face with the masses and settle the problem of abnormal relations that have existed between cadres and masses for many years.

Since the 10th plenum of the Central Committee, the directives of the Central Committee on socialist education have been well carried out in many places. Not only has the "tendency of going it alone" been checked, but the cover has been taken off the class struggle in the rural areas, various kinds of contradictions exposed, and many evil elements engaged in sabotaging socialism uncovered. At the Central Committee meeting in February of this year, Comrade Mao Tse-tung introduced the successful experience attained in Hunan and Hopei provinces. He said: "Once class struggle is grasped, miracles are possible." At first, cadres and Party comrades in many localities did not concentrate on socialist education work. They failed to grasp the essential points or find the correct method. After the February meeting, however, they succeeded in mastering socialist education work, grasping the essential points and finding the correct method. An example is found in Honan province, where the work of socialist education has been carried out with good results. In Honan, they have even made good use of combining the history of the revolutionary struggles of their own communes and brigades, the history of agrarian reform, and the history of collectivization to remind the older generation of the suffering they sustained under the oppression of the exploiting class, and the sufferings under the exploitation of the landlords and rich peasants, thereby arousing their class sentiments. With this method, they also have made the younger generation realize the fact that the fruits of revolutionary struggles did not come easily. The youngsters were made to pore over the "family record" of the proletariat. Thus, the class awakening of the poor peasants and the lower-middle peasants has been heightened, the positiveness of their attitude quickly put to good use, and as they become resolutely determined to break with capitalism and feudalism it has become possible swiftly to organize a class army.

As shown by the experience of Honan province, socialist education in the rural areas can be carried out in three steps: first, devote some 20 days to train a group of cadres; second, train more cadres and active elements among the poor and lower-middle peasants; third, start the all-out efforts. When taking these steps, "spot testing" is a necessary process. The Central Committee is of the conviction that this method of carrying out the work by dividing it into steps and subjecting it to spot testing is correct. The experiences of Honan province and those of the Northeast are included in the 20 appendices of this resolution. As regards this type of socialist education work, successful experience has also been gained in other places. Their experiences must be consolidated and reviewed diligently. In all places, efforts must be made to adopt appropriate methods based on the experiences and on the actual conditions of the locality, and the work of socialist education must be further developed with diligence.

VII. THE PROBLEM OF HOW TO ORGANIZE A REVOLUTIONARY CLASS ARMY

The work of socialist education should be carried out together with the work of organizing the poor and the lower-middle peasants in the rural areas. Poor peasants in Hunan province have correctly said: "If it were not for the fact that we peasants have been organized, the landlords would not have been so honest." They were also right in saying: "During the past years when the poor and lower-middle peasants were not organized, we were like pearls without a string, or leaves torn from the branches."

In the two years following the 1960 movement for the rectification of cadre work styles and the readjustment of the communes, Hopei province successively set up a large number of organizations of the poor and lower-middle peasants. After having gone through socialist education following the Central Committee's tenth plenum, the province took another step forward to strengthen those organizations and continued the establishment of more organizations of the poor and lower-middle peasants.

The Central Committee is of the conviction that in order to strengthen the proletariat dictatorship and the collective economy, and to develop agricultural production, the work of setting up organizations of the poor and lower-middle peasants in the rural collective economic system is wholly essential.

Organizations of the poor and the lower-middle peasants should be set up at three levels—the commune, the brigade, and the production team. They should start with the basic accounting units. Educational work should be consolidated in organizations already established and efforts should be exerted to improve such organizations. In places where such organizations are not yet established, efforts should be made to create favorable conditions based on class education and socialist education so that, with plans and leadership, such organizations can be set up in groups at different periods.

Members of organizations of the poor peasants and lower-middle peasants should be the poor and lower-middle peasants of the time of agrarian reform and agricultural collectivization. When the organizations are first established, it is necessary to see to it that the foundation of the new organizations is firmly laid. No corrupt elements, thieves, speculators, and degenerates should be admitted; those who used to gang-up with landlords, rich peasants, counter-revolutionaries and undesirable elements should be barred. Admittance of these branded elements is permissible only when they have made frank confessions and accounted for their evil doings, "washed their hands and bodies," or when they have been proved to have truly corrected their wrongs at mass meetings of the poor and lower-middle peasants. On the other hand, it is not permissible to use pretexts to deliberately bar the poor and lower-middle peasants who have committed minor errors in their daily life. This is to say that in the course of setting up such organizations of the poor and the lower-middle peasants, attention should be paid to the purity as well as the mass nature of the organizations.

Delegates, committees, and chairmen of organizations of the poor and lower-middle peasants should all be elected from among poor and lower-middle peasants.

It is necessary to bring into full play the function of the poor and lower-middle peasant organizations in assisting and overseeing the work of the commune and brigade administrative committees. The committees of poor and lower-middle peasant organizations may appoint their delegates to sit in the administrative committees of the communes and brigades as observers. All important commune and brigade affairs should be discussed with them so that they will understand them. Attempts to exclude them are not permissible. However, care must also be taken that the poor and lower-middle peasant organizations not be allowed to take over the day-to-day affairs of the commune and brigade administrative committees to the extent of obstructing their basic duties. None of the leading elements of poor and lower-middle peasant organizations shall receive any work-point subsidies.

VIII. THE "FOUR CLEANS" PROBLEM

When cadres of the Paoting special district committee in Hopei went to conduct rural village investigations, they found that the peasants had an urgent demand that communes and brigades do a serious job of cleaning-up account books, cleaning-up granaries, cleaning-up properties, and cleaning-up work-points (called Four Cleans in short). Today the contradiction of Four Uncleans is prevalent in the communes and brigades. This is principally a contradiction between the cadres and the masses. It should be resolved, and it is not difficult to solve. Hence, the Paoting special district committee has wholeheartedly provided leadership for Four Cleans work. Furthermore, it has treated Four Cleans work as constituting a new stage in carrying out socialist education.

The report of the Paoting committee said:

> Four Cleans is like a magic mirror [that reveals monsters]. Whether one is a just or false official becomes immediately clear. Thus our work has a better foundation. Cadres who have been guilty of all kinds of deficiencies and errors undergo discussion and can review their errors and shed their burdens. Thus with a clear conscience, they can speedily and happily "take a warm bath" and an "inoculation" against future errors. A small number of cadres who have committed relatively serious mistakes have also expressed their determination to repent. If the cadres sincerely review their errors and actively make compensation, they generally are forgiven by the masses—except for a few bad elements and those in whom the masses have completely lost confidence. The masses say: "The cadres work all year for the commune members. If their mistakes are corrected, it is all right." The cadres shed their burdens, the masses are relieved, and both cadres and masses are more closely united.

This experience is an important one: it should be broadened.

What the Paoting committee calls Four Cleans is sometimes called Three, Five, or Six Cleans in other places. Actually the substance is about the same. No matter how many Cleans it is called, what the peasants are most concerned about are clean accounts and clean working-points. Since collectivization, a considerable number of communes and brigades have never been able to clean their accounts and work-points, or have always handled them in a perfunctory way.

Now, the first thing to be done is to set the masses in motion to conduct an all-out, thorough check of accounts, warehouses, properties, and work-points starting from last year to the present. This investigation should include the assets procured with state investments, bank loans and proceeds accrued from credit sales of the business departments. This will be a large-scale movement of the masses coordinated with socialist education, its principal purpose being the resolution of internal contradictions of the people. And as far as the corrupt elements, thieves, speculators and degenerates are concerned, it will be a very serious class struggle.

Like the Five-Anti movement now going on in the cities, the rural Four Cleans campaign is a socialist revolutionary struggle that will deal a smashing blow to the frenzied attack of the capitalists. The completion and victory of these two movements will undoubtedly mean another big step forward in the socialist construction enterprise of our country.

This is the policy of our Party: education by persuasion; washing hands and bodies; going to the front with a light load; unity against the enemy. By unity against the enemy, we mean unity of more than 95 percent of the masses and of more than 95 percent of the cadres for the struggle against the class enemy and nature. Evil doings exposed as a result of the Movement should be carefully analyzed. They should be dealt with individually on the basis of their different conditions. The methods of disposition should differ in accordance with the different degree of their seriousness.

The principal objective is education rather than punishment—which is only supplementary. Actual punishment is to be meted out to those for whom punishment is considered imperative by both the masses and the leadership. For those comrades who have committed minor errors or have shortcomings of a general nature, sincere assistance should be extended to help them "wash hands and bodies" and redeem themselves and work with renewed efforts. Nevertheless, all money taken illegally through corruption or theft, and all other property that should be retrieved, must be returned and accounted for. The point must be reached where all cadres must be "clean of hand and foot." No slipshod attitude can be tolerated. Of course, reasonableness should be observed in retrieving the stolen cash and goods. As long as the matter has been straightened out, the masses naturally will not make excessive demands.

This Four Cleans movement represents a serious test to all cadres both within and without the Party who are not "clean of hand and foot." Through this test, they can choose between honestly "washing their hands and bodies" so as to advance with a light load on their conscience, or remaining unawakened in their wrongs, sinking ever deeper until they become degenerates. This is a high hurdle that must be surmounted before entering the state of socialism. All such cadres must be made to understand that "being clean" is a must; that they must clean themselves of their own accord rather than be compelled to do so; that since it must be done, they had better do it earlier; and that it would be useless to take chances and try to get away with it. It should be noted that the great majority of our comrades are good. Although some of them have committed minor errors, they can reform successfully with assistance from the masses and the leadership. Efforts therefore must be made to unite such comrades to do the work well so that we can advance another step forward in isolating opposing elements.

To assure this movement of strong leadership, we must rely on the organizations of the poor and lower-middle peasants; we must do the job well in conducting investigation and research on the masses; and we must set the masses in motion. Decisions for and disposition of all important problems must be made through full discussions among the masses. During the course of the movement, the masses must be given the opportunity fully to express their views, to make criticism of errors and shortcomings, to expose bad people and evil deeds. Efforts, however, must be made to prevent compulsory confession; physical punishment of any sort should be strictly prohibited. Those criticized must be given the chance to defend themselves, so as to allow the masses by democratic process to determine the validity of their defense.

In dealing with the corrupt elements and thieves, the struggle meeting method should not be employed for most cases. Instead, the "back-to-back" method can be adopted. When necessary, mass meetings of a smaller scale can be held to try the accused. At the same time, ad hoc teams can carry out investigations and research on the case. Thereafter, verdicts can be made on the basis of the evidence gathered. Corruption and theft cases of a serious nature, upon consent of the masses at discussions, may be tried and disposed of through legal procedures. Concerning those units whose leadership nucleus has serious defects, or those units whose leading cadres are too weak in leadership, their superior authorities should send appropriate personnel to bolster their leadership. This Movement must be carried out with the cadres group by group. It must be carried out truly and thoroughly. Any perfunctory manner must be strictly precluded. Also to be prevented is the habit of procrastination. Those who have gone through the Movement should be reinvestigated. The Movement should be repeated where it has not been carried out thoroughly and diligently. Some essential systems should be established for places where such systems are absent.

In future, publication shall be made periodically of all items of accounts as stipulated in the 60 Articles. In addition, extensive inventory shall be made once or twice annually. This shall make the Four Cleans a permanent system for the people's communes, the brigades, and the production teams, starting first with the basic accounting units. It shall also be an important part of the Socialist Education Movement.

In order to provide good leadership for all these tasks, first-level hsien cadres should combine their work with the Five-Anti movement for the purpose of checking on and improving the leadership and the manner of carrying out the work. Those who are "unclean of hands and feet" must first "wash their hands and bodies," "dump their burdens," and correct their class standpoint and ideological manner. Only thus can a strong central leadership be established at the top level of a hsien. Only thus can all strength be concentrated to give effective leadership in carrying out all the important tasks.

IX. THE PROBLEM OF CADRES JOINING THE COLLECTIVE PRODUCTION LABOR FORCE

Ours is a party of the proletariat, an advanced political party of the laboring masses. We must place the root organizations of our Party in the hands of the active, advanced elements of the labor masses. The secretaries of the Party branches in rural areas must be not only the most advanced elements in politics, but also the most advanced among the labor masses. They should strive to be good hands in production work, to be models of labor.

Comrade Mao Tse-tung, in his comments on seven items of data concerning labor participation by cadres of Chekiang province, pointed out on May 9, 1963, that the massive body of cadres, especially the cadres on the four levels of hsien, commune, brigade, and production team, must possess a deep awareness of the great revolutionary meaning of their participation in collective production labor.

Comrade Mao Tse-tung said: "We hope to succeed within three years in having all the Party secretaries in the rural Party branches throughout the country devote themselves to participation in production labor. If we succeed in having one-third of all the secretaries in the Party branches join in the production labor during the first year, we will have scored a great victory."

To have the secretaries of Party branches participate in collective production labor in accordance with the established system will indicate that the cadres of our Party are ordinary laborers as well, and not overlords who sit above the heads of the people. By participating in the collective production labor, the secretaries of Party branches will be able to maintain extensive, constant, and intimate contacts with the masses. They will be able promptly to understand the relations between classes, the problems of the masses, and the production situation; to undertake timely consultations with the masses; and through the mass line settle the problems. Cadres at the basic level who do not take part in collective production labor are often unable to provide a correct reflection of the true situation.

The secretary of a rural Party branch in Chekiang province said: "Being good at labor is the only way to achieve good work; without joining in labor, one's work will be like duckweed floating on water, unable to reach the bottom."

The masses of Hsiyang hsien in Shansi province had this comment to make on the cadres' participation in the production labor: "Cadres who joined in the production labor are able to see and hear for themselves, to do what has to be done and say what needs saying. In such a case, how can production be bad?"

These remarks are all correct and appropriate.

To have the cadres participate diligently in collective production labor in accordance with the established system is, from the standpoint of the socialist system, a great matter of fundamental importance. Cadres who do not participate in collective production labor are apt to divorce themselves from the broad laboring masses, thereby making it possible for revisionism to emerge.

In addition to taking the lead in collective production labor, the secretaries of Party branches should also make efforts to educate the cadres at the various commune levels, to drive home the conviction that doing good work is not enough, that doing well in labor is also a must, and that both work and labor must not be neglected.

In order to ensure that secretaries of the Party will have the necessary time to join in collective labor each year, the various leading organs at the commune level and higher must truly try to make their meetings brief whenever possible. Avoid holding all unnecessary meetings. If a meeting is necessary, full preparations should be made beforehand. Prior to convening a meeting, all problems that need solution should be brought out in order that the cadres can exchange their views accordingly. Wherever possible and necessary, meetings may be held at the lower echelons. They can even be held at the work sites and in the paddy fields. In this way, not only the frequency of meetings and the time they consume can be drastically cut down, the effectiveness of the meetings in solving problems will also be greatly enhanced. Cadres above the hsien and commune levels should diligently endeavor to improve the methods to lead and raise the level of their leadership.

Cadres at the hsien, commune, and higher levels should also persist in executing the resolutions promulgated on September 25, 1958 by the Party Central Committee and the State Council concerning the participation by cadres in physical labor. The Central Committee on March 23, 1963 has already approved and passed on for circulation the report submitted by the provincial Party committee of Shansi concerning the insistence by cadres in Hsiyang hsien in joining in production labor on a long-term basis. If the cadres of Hsiyang hsien are able to persist in joining in production labor on a long-term basis, there is no reason why cadres in other hsien cannot do the same.

X. The Problem of Marxism's Scientific Methods of Carrying Out Investigation and Research

Facts prove that there are many problems which are not only not difficult to discover, but are also not difficult to solve. What is important is whether or not our comrades can get close to the masses, whether or not they can carry out investigation and research work, and whether or not they are able to concentrate the diverse opinions among the masses, form systematic opinions, and obtain unified recognition among leading cadres through fermentation and discussion. In addition to the most convenient method for understanding conditions, i.e., participating in collective production labor, responsible comrades of Party organizations at various levels must also in a planned and selective manner squat at points, humbly listen to the opinions of the masses, discover problems in good time, and summarize experiences.

In recent years, the Party Central Committee has once again raised problems of investigation and research. The responsible comrades of some Party organizations diligently carried out the Party Central Committee's directives. They did not make observations in a hurried manner. They did not wander about aimlessly, nor did they lend their ears to mere gossip and rumors. They did not select superficial, one-sided particular material for the purpose of pleading a case for their own subjective designs; on the contrary they really went deeply into the basic levels and squatted, and obtained systematic and fundamental knowledge about important problems. In this manner they quickly improved their work and pushed it forward by big strides. However, some comrades did not act in this manner; they talked about investigation and research, but they lacked enthusiasm, the determination to train their eyes on the lower levels, and the thirst for the spirit of small schoolboys toward learning. Therefore, they were unable to do or do well any investigation and research work. In his "Preface to *Rural Surveys*," Comrade Mao Tse-tung said: "We must clearly understand that the masses are the real heroes, while we ourselves are often childish and ignorant, and without this understanding it is impossible to acquire even the most rudimentary knowledge." On this point, it is true that toward certain comrades it is still necessary to shout loudly. At present, we still have some comrades in leading work posts, and many comrades engaged in general work, who do not understand, or do not quite understand, the scientific and revolutionary epistemology of Marxism. Their world view and methodology is bourgeois or still has remnants of bourgeois ideology. Consciously or unconsciously, they often substitute subjectivism (idealism) for materialism, metaphysics for dialectics. Since this is so, their investigation and research work cannot be done well. In order to do our work well, Party committees at various levels should make great efforts to promote the study of Marxist epistemology, to make it the epistemology of the masses, and put it in the grasp of the broad number of cadres and the masses of people. Philosophy should be liberated from the classes and books of philosophers, and turned into a sharp weapon in the hands of the masses.

*　　　*　　　*

The above listed ten issues are basic questions confronting our current rural work. They concern basic ideological, political, organizational and economic aspects of the establishment of our Party. They are issues decisive in determining who triumphs over whom in the struggle between socialism and capitalism. They concern the question of who wins in the struggle of Marxism and Leninism against revisionism. The reliable way to solve these ten questions is for us to rely on the large body of masses and cadres, to make use of the self-education method, to make the communes a success. Total solution, or even basic solution, of these ten issues will amount to full success in our work of basically revamping the Party's rural organizations at the basic level. It is requested that all bureaus of the Central Committee, all Party committees of the various provinces, cities, and districts, and all local and hsien committees give these ten issues top priority in their studies and research. It is also requested that all related activities be well planned in advance, well deployed as a whole. We must grasp the opportunities firmly in our hands. Under the condition that production not be deferred and that all undertakings be closely coordinated with production, we must break down the work for solving these ten problems into phases and sectors and carry it out with well-planned steps. We must strive for total accomplishment of this work in three years and energetically seek to do a good job.

The Party's Central Committee hereby calls upon comrades of the Party to learn and to comprehend this directive of extraordinary importance issued recently by Comrade Mao Tse-tung:

Class struggle, production struggle, and scientific experiment are the three great revolutionary movements that build up a powerful socialist nation. They are a guarantee for the Communists to do away with bureaucratism, to avoid revisionism and dogmatism, to stand eternally invincible. They are an assurance for the proletariat to be able to unite with the massive labor populace in order to realize democratic dictatorship of the proletariat. Otherwise, the landlords, the rich peasants, the counter-revolutionaries, the bad elements and the evils would all come out; our comrades would do nothing about it, and many people would even resort to collusion without distinguishing friend from foe, and thereby allow the enemy to erode and invade, to divide and dissolve, to abduct and penetrate. Many workers, peasants and intellectuals would then become prey to enemy tactics of coupling force with inducement. If things were allowed to go on this way, the day would not be too far off—few years, over ten years, or few decades at the most—when the resurgence of a nation-wide counter-revolution becomes inevitable. It would then become a certainty that the Party of Marxism and Leninism would turn into a party of revisionism, of Fascism. The whole of China would then change color. Let all fellow comrades give it a thought. Isn't that a most dangerous situation!

. . . This Socialist Education Movement is a great revolutionary movement. It not only covers the problem of class struggle, but also includes the question of cadres joining in production labor. It also embodies the kind of work in which one will learn how to solve a group of problems in enterprises and industries through experiments with a strict scientific attitude. This may seem very difficult. Actually, all that is required is diligence, and the solution will not be difficult to find. This is a struggle that calls for the re-education of man. This is a struggle for reorganizing the revolutionary class armies for a confrontation with the forces of feudalism and capitalism which are now feverishly attacking us. We must nip their counter-revolution in the bud. We must make it a great movement to reform the bulk of elements in these counter-revolutionary forces and turn them into new men. With cadres and masses joining hand-in-hand in the production labor and scientific experiments, our Party will take another stride forward in becoming a more glorious, greater, and more correct party; our cadres will be versed in politics as well as in business operations, become red as well as expert. They will then no longer be toplofty, no longer bureaucrats and overlords, no longer divorced from the masses. They will then merge themselves with the masses, becoming truly good cadres supported by the masses. When this educational movement is completed, there will emerge throughout the nation a new climate for progress into greater prosperity. When this climate has emerged for a nation with one-fourth the population of the entire earth, our contributions toward internationalism will be even greater.

Party comrades, let us all unite together under the great banner of Comrade Mao Tse-tung!

APPENDIX C* (THE LATER TEN POINTS)

SOME CONCRETE POLICY FORMULATIONS OF THE CENTRAL COMMITTEE OF THE CHINESE COMMUNIST PARTY IN THE RURAL SOCIALIST EDUCATION MOVEMENT †

(Draft, September 1963)

The "Draft Resolution on Some Problems in Current Rural Work," which was issued by the Central Committee in May of this year, is a great document with guiding authority. It is an important document on the basic reconstruction of our Party in the ideological, political, organizational and economic aspects.

This document deals with ten problems, greatly supplementing the contents of the Socialist Education Movement which has been carried on in various rural villages since the tenth plenary session of the eighth Central Committee.

Since June of this year, various Central Committee bureaus and departments, and Party Committees of various provinces, municipalities and autonomous regions have made preparations for launching a large-scale rural socialist education movement. On the one hand, they have called cadres to meetings of various kinds to train the cadres; on the other they have made "spot testings." Some of these "spot testings" have already been concluded; the rest are soon to be concluded. Experiences gained in such spot-testings have amply proved that Comrade Mao Tse-tung's analyses and instructions on such problems as classes, class contradictions and class struggle in a socialist society, have great revolutionary and historic significance. They have also fully proved that this Socialist Education Movement, launched in accordance with Comrade Mao's instructions, has long-range and far-reaching significance in repulsing the frantic offensive of the once loudly aggressive imperialist and feudalist forces, in consolidating the position of rural socialist and proletarian dictatorship, in destroying the social basis from which revisionism stems, in consolidating collective economy, and in developing agricultural production. At the same time, in spot-testings at various places, a number of problems concerning concrete policies have been brought out. These problems must be solved so that the "Draft Resolution on Some Problems in Rural Work" can be further implemented. The following are formulations concerning these concrete policies.

I. BASIC DIRECTIONS AND MAIN CONTENTS OF THE SOCIALIST EDUCATION MOVEMENT

The Rural Socialist Education Movement now being pushed is an important socialist revolutionary movement. Comrade Mao Tse-tung has wisely and clearly explained the great significance of the Movement. He said:

> The Socialist Education Movement is a great revolutionary movement, which involves not only the question of class struggle but also the ques-

---

* Acknowledgment is made of a translation in *Issues & Studies*, Institute of International Relations, Taipei, Vol. II, Nos. 9 and 10 (June and July, 1966) pp. 34–44 and 36–48 respectively. This translation has been checked against the Chinese text and some editorial revisions made by the authors and staff of the Center for Chinese Studies.

† *Chung-kung chung-yang kuan-yü nung-ts'un she-hui chiao-yü yün-tung chung i-hsieh chü-t'i cheng-ts'e ti kuei-ting (ts'ao-an).*

tion of cadre participation in physical labor. It also includes such work as learning to solve a number of problems in enterprises and undertakings by adopting strict scientific methods and experiments.

He also said:

This struggle is one for the re-education of men; for the reorganization of revolutionary class force to wage sharp and effective struggles against the forces of capitalism and feudalism which are launching an audacious attack upon us; it is a great movement to suppress their counter-revolutionary activities and to remold the majority of these elements into new men; it is also a campaign for the joint participation of cadres and the masses in productive labor and scientific experiments, with a view to bringing our Party a step further in becoming a more glorious, greater and more correct Party, and making our cadres well-versed in politics and in business operations, both red and expert, well integrated with and supported by the masses, instead of being divorced from the masses and considering themselves officials and overlords. After the completion of this education movement, there will emerge in the whole country a climate of brightness and prosperity. With the appearance of such a climate among a population constituting almost one-fourth of the whole population of the world, our contribution to internationalism will be even greater.

In accordance with Comrade Mao Tse-tung's instructions, this movement should grasp five basic points. They are: class struggle, socialist education, organization of the poor and lower-middle peasants, "four cleans," and participation of cadres in collective labor. Of the five, class struggle is the most basic. The key to and prerequisite of correctly launching and leading the Socialist Education Movement is to study Comrade Mao Tse-tung's thought concerning such questions as classes, class contradiction and class struggle in a socialist society, and then to clearly understand and remember his thoughts. To take up class struggle as a principle, to grasp five vital points, to mobilize the masses freely and systematically and, with good leadership, to consolidate over 95 percent of the masses and cadres to repulse the offensive of capitalist and feudalistic forces, to heighten the socialist consciousness and class consciousness of cadres and masses, to readjust the basic organizations in the rural villages, to strengthen and consolidate the collective economy and to develop agricultural production—all these are basic policies for this Socialist Education Movement.

During this movement, we must systematically carry out the following 12 items of work:

1) Organize and train work teams. This job must be truly well done. To ensure the capability of the teams, their members must be recruited through strict selection and screening. Anyone having serious mistakes exposed during the Five-Anti movement who has not yet made serious confession and self-examination should be barred from joining the work teams. Members of the teams must all study with seriousness the instructions of Comrade Mao Tse-tung, seriously study the Draft Resolution on Some Problems in Current Rural Work issued by the Central Committee, the present draft policy decisions, and other related documents issued by the Central Committee.

2) Convoke three-level cadre meetings and cadre meetings of the people's communes, to repeatedly study Comrade Mao Tse-tung's instructions, the Draft Resolution on Some Problems in Current Rural Work issued by the Central Committee, and the draft policy in this document, and to read to the public typical materials concerning the Socialist Education Movement of other places in conjunction with exposures of the situation of local class

struggle in order to carry out class education and policy education. Representatives of poor and lower-middle peasants may be recruited to participate in such meetings. Through such meetings, the majority of cadres who have committed common mistakes or more serious mistakes can be made to voluntarily "wash hands and take baths" and discard their "burdens," so as to take the first steps in forming a leading group. In such meetings, the situation and implementation of the 60 Articles should also be examined. Reviews and investigations should be made whenever there is violation of the 60 Articles.

3) Mobilize and organize poor and lower-middle peasants through visits to the poor and the suffering, and contacting and taking deep root among these masses. Members of the working teams should eat, live and work together with these poor and lower-middle peasants as much as they can.

4) Convoke Party meetings at the basic levels, such as the commune committee meetings, commune branch meetings, and commune small group meetings, thus carrying out class education, criticism and self-criticism among the Party members, and helping Party members who have gone astray to recognize and correct their mistakes.

5) Mobilize the masses, especially the poor and lower-middle peasant masses, and call meetings at the production team, production brigade and commune levels, to carry forward the Four Cleans in order to do a good job in ideological education and improve cadres' consciousness. Such problems as retrieving misappropriated money from the cadres or making them repay what has been misused should be handled correctly.

6) Educate the masses in socialism, collectivism, patriotism, and internationalism. Draw a clear demarcation line between capitalism and socialism, and solve the problems of the relationship between the public and the private, and the struggle between the two lines of capitalism and socialism. Educate the masses in the correct handling of the relations between the state, the collective, and the individual, and positively carry out production plans and the mission of the sale of agricultural sidelines entrusted them. Toward those who are detrimental to the interests of collective economy, who have enthusiastically developed "small freedoms," and who are enthusiastic in business of their own but do not positively participate in collective production, education by persuasion should be carried out, so as to heighten their consciousness and make them voluntarily remedy mistakes. To those members who have shown more serious voluntary inclination toward capitalism, appropriate criticisms should be made. Those who have always shown their love of the collective, who positively participate in labor, and who stick to the line of socialism, should be commended.

7) Educate the masses in class struggle. Draw a clear line between friends and foes. Mobilize the masses to carry out the persuasion struggle against the enemy. Handle with care the four elements engaged in destructive activities, elements engaged in speculation and profiteering, and elements who are corrupt and plundering.

8) Establish organizations of poor and lower-middle peasants.

9) Readjust basic units of the Party, the Young Communist League and the Women's Association, militia, and other rural organizations.

10) Re-elect or transfer cadres of the communes, production brigades, and teams.

11) Establish a sound system for the participation of cadres in collective production labor.

12) Further consolidate collective economy on the basis of heightening of class consciousness and positiveness in the collective production of cadres and

masses. In accordance with stipulations of the 60 Articles, improve the management and administration of production teams, improve the management and administration of commune enterprises and production brigades, map out and improve various systems, and draw plans for the development of production by the production teams, production brigades and the communes.

The 12 items of work listed above constitute the main contents of this Socialist Education Movement. They are inter-related and mutually supplementary, and may be carried out simultaneously or seriatim, in accordance with different local situations and experience gained in spot-testings. But all should be carried out effectively. Only by so doing can the Socialist Education Movement be brought to a successful conclusion. This is our common experience.

The Socialist Education Movement now being pushed is a large-scale mass movement even more complicated than the land reform movement. It involves many problems and influences a broad scope, and will result in a very sharp struggle. Comrade Mao Tse-tung has repeatedly instructed us that this Movement should be carried out by stages, and that it is permissible that within a locality the work is carried out with different priority and results. In accordance with this instruction of Comrade Mao Tse-tung, Party committees of various provinces, municipalities and autonomous regions have all made concrete preparations for carrying out this Movement in their respective localities. Generally speaking, the thorough completion of this Movement in rural villages of the whole country will probably require two to three years.

II. Problems to be Emphasized in Leading the Socialist Education Movement

The key to the questions of whether the Socialist Education Movement can be carried out smoothly, and whether the Party's policies can be carried out correctly in the Movement, lies in the leadership. Leading organizations on provincial, district and hsien levels must pay close attention to the following points:

1) Leading the "hand-washing" and "bathing." Cadres of provincial, district and hsien leading organizations, especially major leading cadres, must first "wash hands" and "take a bath." They must first correct their class stand and improve their thinking and work style before they can lead in the smooth carrying out of the Socialist Education Movement. Otherwise, it will be impossible for them to do so. Some of the leading cadres have unclean hands and feet, and the masses have lost their respect for them. When such cadres ask their subordinates to carry out the Four Cleans, they cannot possibly expect good results.

Therefore, all cadres at provincial, district, and hsien levels should first participate in the Five-Anti movement. In hsien-level organizations where the Five-Anti movement has not yet been carried out, about ten days should be spent on the convocation of three level cadres' meetings, in order to cause cadres of department or bureau chief level and higher to "wash hands and take a bath," discard their "burdens" and "go to the front lightly equipped."

2) Leadership responsibility and personal participation in work. Important leading personnel at the provincial, special district and hsien levels must personally carry out spot testing in order to obtain experiences, set examples, and direct and push forward the entire Movement. It is not proper only to give orders and not participate in work, or, although personally "taking command," to avoid actual participation in work. After the Movement is launched, leading personnel must at all times pay attention to carrying out investigation

and research in order to discover and solve problems in good time. It is also improper to be satisfied merely with listening to reports at meetings and reading written materials, and not go deeply into the lower levels to make a substantial examination. During the course of the whole Movement, leading organs must regularly summarize experiences. Only in this way can they take account of the overall situation rather than proceeding in a halting manner. Only in this way can the level of the cadres continually be raised and the direction of the Movement continually be strengthened.

3) Carrying on delicate work and deeply mobilizing the masses. During the process of this Movement, the Central Committee draft resolutions' demand that "the work must be practically and truly carried out group by group; perfunctoriness must be strictly prevented" must be carried out conscientiously. As soon as the Movement is started, Comrade Mao Tse-tung's instructions and the Central Committee's policies should be directly introduced to the cadres and masses, and repeatedly expounded to make them known to every household. Thus the Central Committee's policies can be grasped by the cadres and masses and turned into action. During the process of the Movement, either in organizing class ranks, in carrying out the Four Cleans, or in launching struggles against the enemy, the masses must be widely mobilized, so as to make the Movement a true revolutionary struggle of self-awakened masses. Work must be carried out with care. Carelessness must be strictly prevented. All arrangements must be given ample time for implementation. According to our experience, to complete this Socialist Education Movement on a "spot" will require probably three months. It would be improper to try to complete the whole work of Socialist Education Movement within ten days or half a month. It would be hard to avoid troubles and failures.

4) Rely on the basic organizations and basic cadres. In the Socialist Education Movement, it would obviously be wrong for the work teams to work in circles within the basic cadres, without making contact and taking deep root among and mobilizing the poor and lower-middle peasant masses. However, it would be equally wrong for them to brush aside the basic organizations and existing cadres, instead of carrying out work by relying upon them. This method of doing things would create an opposition between the basic-level cadres on the one hand and the work team and poor and lower-middle peasants on the other, thereby undermining the smooth development of the Movement. The main mission of the work team is to serve as "staff" of the basic-level cadres, to draw plans, carry out guidance and assistance, and enlighten the basic-level cadres in the analysis of problems and the determination of policies and methods. But they should never monopolize nor take the place of the basic-level cadres. As for the communes and brigades whose leadership has been usurped by landlords, rich peasants, counter-revolutionaries and undesirable elements, or those communes and brigades which are being controlled by degenerates, the situation is different. After investigations have proved the existence of such communes and brigades, and upon approval of the hsien Party committee, capable work teams should be dispatched to such communes and brigades to take the places of those bad cadres. The poor and lower-middle peasants should be directly mobilized to carry out rectification and regularization, to cultivate positive elements, and gradually to form a new leading nucleus. Of course, attention still should be paid to the consolidation of some good or basically good Party members and cadres of these communes and brigades, and carry out the work together with them.

5) Further implementation of the Movement. All problems related to the 60 Articles should be handled strictly in accordance with the stipulations of

the 60 Articles. The 60 Articles should in no case be put aside and new methods adopted. Whether the 60 Articles have been well implemented should be a yardstick in judging the result of the Socialist Education Movement.

6) Close connection with production work. Before the Socialist Education Movement is launched, the cadres are apt to lay too much emphasis on production and to neglect the class struggle. After the Movement is launched, especially after the masses are mobilized, they are apt to ignore the production work. These two discrepancies should both be avoided. The development of the Socialist Education Movement should be closely coordinated and connected with the production work. At no stage of the Movement should production be affected. And measures taken during the course of the Movement should be helpful to production. During the whole process of the Movement, attention should be paid at all times to the channeling of the masses' political enthusiasm and labor positiveness, to the consolidation of the collective economy and the development of agricultural production (including the collective sideline occupations).

7) Integration of point and broad plane. Socialist education work on the plane should be positively accomplished. Work on the point, which should be done with great care, will take considerably longer to finish—about three months. Work on the plane, including the checking of the evil influences, mobilization of the masses, preliminary regulation of the masses-cadres relationship, and dealing preliminary blows to the class enemy, requires around twenty days only. The reason that point and plane should be connected is that this Socialist Education Movement is being developed from point to the plane and step by step. At any particular time, a majority of the communes and brigades are temporarily not systematically engaged in the Movement. Pushing the Movement on the points will certainly have a great impact on the plane. If we relax our efforts on the vast plane, serious losses will result.

On the plane, in addition to keeping a firm grasp of daily work, the following items should also be well carried out:

(a) With district or commune as a unit, convene three level or four level cadre meetings. All Party members and representatives of poor and lower-middle peasants should be called upon to participate, and to study the draft resolution of the Central Committee and the draft of these policy formulations. The duration of the meetings should be around ten days. Participants should be made to understand the directives, policy and aim of this Movement, and to heighten consciousness and dispel anxieties. Later, they should be relied upon to carry out widespread and far-reaching publicity among the masses, in order to wield influence.

(b) Teach basic-level cadres to understand the significant meaning of relying upon the poor and lower-middle peasants. On the plane it is not necessary to set up organizations of poor and lower-middle peasants in a hurry; but the convocation of meetings of poor and lower-middle peasants can be used to commence various activities. Positive assistance should be given to poor and lower-middle peasants who have troubles in production and living, to help them solve their problems.

(c) Encourage voluntary correction of defects and mistakes by the cadres, so that they may go into battle with a lighter burden and be united in fighting the enemy; demand the unification and division of labor, the cleaning up of work points and accounts, and the establishment of necessary systems of the cadres; forbid over-eating, waste and luxury, embezzlement of public funds, corruption and larceny, speculating and profiteering, high-interest loans, beating and scolding the masses and violation of laws and discipline.

(d) Call on cadres to join actively in collective labor and do well in experimental plots, improve ideology and attitude, carry out democratic management of the communes, and closely cooperate with the masses.

(e) Continue propaganda on the implementation of the 60 Articles, strengthen the collective economy and develop rural sideline production.

(f) Guard closely against destructive activities of class enemies. With the brigade as unit, convene meetings of landlords, rich peasants, counter-revolutionaries and undesirable elements and pass on to them policies and rules, telling them to abide by the law and not to commit any destructive activity, and deal hard blows to offenders caught in the act. When it is necessary to organize a mass struggle rally, it should first be approved by the hsien Party committee.

The socialist education work on the plane, though not requiring a very long time, or as careful implementation as the work on the point, covers a vast scope and, since it is without the guidance of the work teams, mistakes are apt to be made if due attention is not paid to leadership. Local Party committees, especially the hsien committees, must firmly grasp the work on the plane, and pay close attention to any changes in the situation, so as to discover and solve problems promptly. It is our prediction that after the preliminary stage of the socialist education work on the plane, there will be discovered some communes and brigades in which the situation is especially serious, the class struggle is particularly sharp and where there are many problems needing speedy solution. Work teams must be dispatched promptly to such communes and brigades and, using each of such communes and brigades as a point, carry out a systematic and penetrative Socialist Education Movement.

III. Consolidate the More Than 95 Percent of the Peasant Masses

The consolidation of over 95 percent of the peasants, as advocated by Comrade Mao Tse-tung, is a basic policy in advancing the Socialist Education Movement.

To truly consolidate over 95 percent of the peasant masses really depends on whether we have firmly and comprehensively implemented the Party's class line in the rural villages. Poor and lower-middle peasants constitute 60 to 70 percent of the rural population. When our work among the poor and lower-middle peasants is satisfactorily completed, there will be sufficient guarantee that consolidation of over 95 percent of the peasants will be successfully carried out.

To consolidate over 95 percent of the peasant masses, we should also distinguish clearly the contradiction between the enemy and ourselves, and the internal contradiction among the people, and correctly handle the internal contradiction among the people, when actually carrying out the policy. To put it a more concrete way, we should be able to distinguish and correctly handle the following questions:

1) We should distinguish between the class enemies planning to stage a come-back, and those backward masses who allow themselves to be utilized by the enemy out of temporary foolishness. Among the peasant masses, there are a small part, including very few poor and lower-middle peasants, who are backward ideologically and are unable to draw a clear line among classes. Under enticement of the enemy, they have either committed some crimes which are detrimental to the state or the collective interests, or have taken part in some feudalistic or superstitious activities. We should not treat such

persons in the same way we do the enemy and deal blows on them. Instead, we should educate them, win them over, and make them wake up and resolutely separate from the class enemies.

2) We should distinguish between speculators and those peasants who show a more serious spontaneous capitalist tendency. Of the peasants, there are a certain number who think of nothing but how to become rich, in disregard of the state and collective interest. To remedy such thinking and acts, education and criticism should be carried out. But they are workers, and any education and criticism are for the purpose of enabling them to walk more firmly on the road to socialism. They are not the target of our blows. The people who should be dealt blows are those very few engaged in serious speculating and profiteering activities, sabotage of the market, accumulation of illegal profits, and leading a parasitic life. To such persons, such punitive measures as retrospective collection of taxes or fines, confiscation and court sentence should be meted out, in accordance with the seriousness of their offense and their manners and attitudes.

3) In the struggle against speculation and profiteering, we should also distinguish between speculative activities and proper activities of marketing and trading, vending of a temporary nature, and small scale peddling. Agricultural by-products produced by collective economic units, and products of the commune members' family sidelines and private plots, unless specially limited by the state, should be allowed to be sold in assigned markets after the task of state purchase is fulfilled. Some legal vending and peddling which are permitted by state policy are convenient to the masses' living and should not be considered as speculation or profiteering. Some people have long been engaged in small-scale business. As long as they do not sell materials prohibited by the state, engage in long-distance shipping and selling, or sabotage the market, they should not be looked upon as speculators or profiteers.

4) We should distinguish between spontaneous capitalism and proper family sideline occupations of commune members. In treating the family sideline occupations of commune members, including the cultivation of private plots and small pieces of uncultivated lands, the stipulation of the 60 Articles should be strictly followed, and no violation is tolerated. In opposing spontaneous capitalism, proper family sideline occupations of commune members should not be impaired or limited, nor as stipulated by the 60 Articles should the private plots and barren lands be confiscated at random. In cases where the area of commune members' private plots or uncultivated land exceed the stipulated size, if the excessive land is of a very small area and does not affect the collective economy, generally no action is called for. If the area in excess of the stipulated size is comparatively large, then persuasive education of the peasant should be carried out, and proper measures taken to put the land under the collective ownership.

The four questions listed above are all important ones which we are apt to confuse in the process of the Socialist Education Movement. Besides, there are other demarcations of our policy lines. For instance, the demarcation between corruption, larceny and petty theft; that between such acts as collecting money by utilizing feudalistic superstition, restoration of feudalistic and family rule and carrying out counter-revolutionary activities on the one hand, and the backward customs, habits and common superstitious acts of the masses on the other; and that between extortion, blackmail, high-interest exploitation and mutual assistance and transactions between friends and relatives. In handling these cases, we should adopt an attitude of practicality, make concrete analyses and take careful measures. We should deal with a problem as it is, without exaggerating or minimizing its importance. Otherwise, we will undermine the policy, harm the masses, and damage the Movement.

When the peasants are found to have defects or to have made mistakes, patient education must be carried out in order to bring about their own awakening, heighten their understanding, and enable them voluntarily to correct themselves. As to those who have committed comparatively serious mistakes, they should be subjected to proper criticisms but the directive of persuasive education should still be strictly observed. Some people take into their own possession collective-owned farming implements and other properties, or state-owned materials. They should be given proper education to make them return these materials and properties voluntarily. Some other people have occupied collective-owned land, and they should also be made to return the land through education. In doing so, reasonable measures should be taken in order to avoid the waste of the crops and the land. A very small number of the poor and lower-middle peasants are comparatively more deeply influenced by capitalism, and have comparatively serious capitalist thinking and behavior. Careful education should be carried out for such persons, to make them walk resolutely on the road of socialism. As long as they earnestly repent, then, upon approval of the masses, we can still rely on them and allow them to take part in the poor or lower-middle peasant organizations.

In carrying out the Socialist Education Movement among the masses to deal with those who have shown defects or committed mistakes, we must apply only the measure of "unity-criticism-unity." No struggle rally, no false accusation, and no beating is allowed. In some places, violation of laws such as careless arrests and use of third degree methods have been discovered. Though those were only isolated cases, we should take them seriously.

Workers, cadres, students, and retired servicemen sent down from the cities to the villages to engage in agricultural production are an important force for building socialist villages and should not be neglected. Many of them have received considerable revolutionary education in the army, in factories, in organizations or schools and have relatively high political consciousness, certain working experience, and cultural knowledge. We must consolidate them and make use of them.

Dependents of officers and men of the People's Liberation Army and public security forces mostly live in rural villages. Good work among the military dependents, therefore, has a significant bearing on the strengthening of the armed forces; and on the enhancing of the consolidation between the military and the government, and between the military and the civilian. In this Movement, we should widely propagandize the support-the-army and treat-the-military-dependents-well policies of the Party and the state, and carefully examine the result of the implementation of these policies. We must educate military dependents to cherish their own reputation, set good examples among the masses, positively join in the collective productive labor, and firmly walk on the road of socialism. We must educate cadres and the masses to respect military dependents, and render proper care to some military dependents having livelihood trouble. Marriages of servicemen should be protected according to the laws of the state.

In the Socialist Education Movement, we have only to adopt the above mentioned directives and measures to be confident in consolidating over 95 percent of the peasant masses to wage a joint struggle against the enemy. As for the remaining less than 5 percent, we should not indiscriminately consider them as targets of our blows. They have committed serious mistakes, some of which even fall into the category of contradictions between the enemy and ourselves. Yet, they are all originally working people, and most of them are somewhat different from the class enemy. So we must do our best to win them over. Among them, those who really call for our blows are those very few who are determined to be the enemy of the people.

IV. Concerning the Organization of Poor and Lower-Middle Peasants

1) Necessary measures to be adopted for establishing organizations of poor and lower-middle peasants include paying visits to the poor and the suffering, taking social root in their midst, expanding small organizations into large ones, and pushing the movement step by step. First to be recruited should be poor and lower-middle peasants with good attitude and laboring capability, high political consciousness, and pure background. As for those poor and lower-middle peasants with more defects, bad political stand and poor laboring capability, they should be recruited, group by group, after education and examination during the process of the Movement. Visits to the poor and the suffering, and taking root in the masses, are the most basic work items in the organization of rural class forces. Meanwhile, to freely mobilize the masses, mainly the poor and lower-middle peasant masses, is a basic work item in carrying out the Socialist Education Movement. Experiences gained in various places have proved that any poor or lower-middle peasant organization which is established without going through these processes, but rather only by administrative order, will exist only nominally and will not function well. Some time ago, in some places, some organizations of poor and lower-middle peasants were set up overnight. Most of these organizations either exist in name only or are seriously impure. For such organizations, readjustment and strengthening efforts should be made.

2) Organizations of poor and lower-middle peasants, as pointed out by the Central Committee's draft resolutions, should retain both their purity and their mass nature. Of the backbone elements in poor and lower-middle peasant organizations (for example, committee members, representatives, and small group leaders), old tenants and poor peasants should constitute the absolute majority, while a certain number of new and old lower-middle peasants should also be included. Also, a certain number of youths and women must be included in the backbone elements of poor and lower-middle peasant organizations. This provision will be helpful in strengthening the work with rural youths and women. When the poor and lower-middle peasant organizations are finally taking shape, efforts should be made to recruit the great majority of poor and lower-middle peasants. Those who should be barred from participation should only be those who have close connections with the four elements, who have committed serious mistakes, and who have been reluctant to repent despite repeated reprimands. In ethnically mixed regions, poor and lower-middle peasants of different ethnic groups should be recruited.

3) Routine work schedules should be set up for the poor and lower-middle peasant organizations. In addition to political movements, such organizations also should function in routine production and construction, in strengthening the collective economy, and in consolidation of the proletarian dictatorship. Through the work system, it should be guaranteed that these organizations will assist and supervise the work of communes, production brigades and production teams, as well as cadres working on these three levels. The administrative committees, when discussing important questions, should invite representatives of poor and lower-middle peasants to sit in the meeting. Commune cadres at various levels should be so educated that they will rely on the

poor and lower-middle peasant organizations for the improvement of the collective economy.

4) Whether the poor and lower-middle peasant organizations can carry out their routine work and whether they can always function effectively is decided by the Party leadership. The Party cell should always be concerned about the work of the poor and lower-middle peasant organizations and extend them necessary assistance. Before any major questions concerning the commune or the brigade are discussed within the Party, the opinions of poor and lower-middle peasant organizations should first be solicited. After these Party discussions, the results should first be passed on to poor and lower-middle peasant organizations, and consultation and discussion had with them. All Party branches in the rural villages should have full understanding of the Party's class line in the villages, and truly learn how to carry out their work along this line.

5) As for the organization of rural class ranks during the period of socialist construction, we have not obtained much experience. In establishing organizations of poor and lower-middle peasants, many concrete problems still remain to be solved. These problems include: what are the proper names for the poor and lower-middle peasant organizations; what missions and powers shall these organizations possess; whether the basic unit of these organizations should be the brigade or the production team; whether cadres of various levels of Party organizations in communes and cadres of the administrative commission can serve concurrently as the leading personnel of these organizations; what is the relationship between these organizations and the Party organizations, and between these organizations and the administrative commission; whether poor and lower-middle peasant organizations should be set up at the hsien level; and whether regular meetings of representatives of poor and lower-middle peasants should be convened at the provincial and district levels. Problems like these must be completely solved. Experiments may be continued in various provinces and municipalities. Central Committee departments in charge of rural work should, basing on experiences gained in various places, draw up regulations in the first half of 1964 governing the organizations of poor and lower-middle peasants.

V. THE MIDDLE PEASANT PROBLEM

The problem of the middle peasants is an important one, and should be correctly handled in the Rural Socialist Education Movement. To firmly consolidate other middle peasants while relying on the poor and lower-middle peasants is the Party's long-range class policy for rural villages.

The question of dealing with the middle peasants mainly concerns dealing with the upper-middle peasants. This has two aspects. One is how to classify the upper-middle peasants, and the other is how to consolidate them.

The upper-middle peasants are a comparatively complex class among the peasants. In the course of practical work, discrepancies are likely to occur in the policy of how to treat this class. Improper handling of the upper-middle peasants often affects the relationship with other middle peasants. In the light of this, the question of whether the upper-middle peasants are correctly handled is also the important question of whether over 95 percent of the peasant masses can be consolidated during the Socialist Education Movement.

What is the standard for defining the upper-middle peasants? This is still not clearly understood by some of our comrades. Some comrades simply use the living standard as the classification yardstick. The result is that some poor peasants and other middle peasants are mistakenly classified as upper-middle peasants. Even peasants whose living standard is raised because of the collective type of living after collectivization are also listed as upper-middle peasants. This is wholly disadvantageous to the work of maneuvering the peasants' positiveness in collective production. This will obstruct production instead of promoting it, and is therefore quite wrong. What we positively encourage is that the vast number of peasants should rely on the collective means of developing and increasing wealth together. What we oppose is only the capitalist line of harming the public for benefiting the private, harming others for benefiting oneself, and enriching a few by making the majority impoverished and bankrupt.

There are also some comrades who use the political attitude as yardstick for the classification of the upper-middle peasants. This is unscientific, and, besides, this standard lacks uniformity and is difficult to control. Often, some poor peasants and other middle peasants who are ideologically backward or who show more political shortcomings are likely to be classified as upper-middle peasants, thus causing confusion and chaos among the ranks of the rural class in villages.

Both of the above methods for classification of the upper-middle peasants therefore are all wrong. The basic standard for this classification should be: possession of comparatively more production facilities and commitment of only minor exploitations. Any poor peasant who has been raised to middle peasant since the land reform should not be classified as a new upper-middle peasant, so long as he has not committed minor exploitations. Poor peasants and other middle peasants whose living standard has been elevated since the collectivization should not be classified as new upper-middle peasants if they neither possess major production facilities nor commit such exploitative activities as extending loans, speculation or profiteering. As for those poor and lower-middle peasants who have enriched themselves with illegal income after the collectivization, their status should also generally remain unchanged.

During the land reform, old middle peasants were generally divided into upper-middle peasants (then called rich middle peasants) and common middle peasants. Now, when class ranks in the villages are being defined, it is necessary to decide which of them are old lower-middle peasants. The so-called "old lower-middle peasants" are those old middle peasants who possessed comparatively fewer production facilities and who had to sell a small amount of labor or borrow small loans, and were consequently living at a comparatively low standard. Among common old middle peasants, those other than the old lower-middle peasants are commonly called middle peasants. These peasants should be distinguished from the old upper-middle peasants because they did not exploit others. Therefore they should not be classified as upper-middle peasants. Meanwhile, they are also different from old lower-middle peasants in that they were self-sufficient economically and generally did not have to sell their labor and were free from exploitation by creditors. They are, therefore, not to be considered a strength to rely upon, but only a strength for consolidation.

In view of the fact that some problems exist at present in the classification of various peasant classes, it is necessary for all comrades engaged in rural work to renew the study of the two documents concerning the classification of rural classes promulgated by the Central Committee in 1933, the supplementary resolutions by the Government Administration Council of 1950, and several new decisions of the Council, so as to improve their understanding and make uniform the standard for class analysis. Of course, this does not mean that a new division of classes is going to take place in rural villages.

During this Movement, except for places where the situation is extraordinary, no reclassification will be made. The class backgrounds in rural villages should be assessed on the basis of classifications carried out during the land reform with the changes of status prior to collectivization taken into account. If there is any one who has been mistakenly classified and asks for correction during the organization of the class ranks, the correction may be duly made in accordance with the spirit of the above-mentioned documents.

The upper-middle peasant is a class with more serious tendency toward capitalism. In rural villages, one important aspect in the struggle between socialism and capitalism is the struggle between the lower-middle peasants' persistent work toward socialism and the upper-middle peasants' move toward capitalism. To deal with the upper-middle peasants' tendency toward capitalism, it is necessary to educate, criticize, and in some more serious cases, carry out necessary struggle measures. Otherwise, their wavering attitude cannot be corrected, their influence among the poor and lower-middle peasants cannot be checked, and the collective economy cannot be consolidated. Yet, they are laborers, and our friends. Therefore, we must endeavor to consolidate them, and enable them to correctly function in production. Since the collectivization more than a decade ago, facts have proved that the great majority of upper-middle peasants are capable of following us on the road of socialism.

We should not indiscriminately oppose the upper-middle peasants. What we oppose are only those ideologies and activities counter to the state, collective, and commune members' interests, committed by the minority of the upper-middle peasants with more serious tendency toward capitalism. We should not indiscriminately deal blows to all upper-middle peasants just because a few of them have taken the lead in demanding "individual operation" and engaged in speculation and profiteering.

The conflict between us and the upper-middle peasants with tendency toward capitalism is still an internal conflict of the people, and should be handled with care. After the poor and lower-middle peasants are mobilized and organized, this problem especially deserves our attention. In opposing a few upper-middle peasants for their tendency toward capitalism, we should only adopt the methods of criticism and education, and should not use the measure of struggle which we adopt against our enemy. We should not deprive them of their rights as commune members, brand those under criticism as capitalists, and, especially, encroach upon their legal profits which they earn by joining in collective labor and earn by laboring more than others. In a few places, some incidents happened in which some upper-middle peasants were subjected to struggle in the same way as landlords during the former land reform. Such incidents should be firmly prevented. To push upper-middle peasants to the side of landlords and rich peasants will be most disadvantageous to us.

VI. UNIFY MORE THAN 95 PERCENT OF RURAL CADRES

During the initial stage of the Socialist Education Movement, Comrade Mao Tse-tung's directives of "persuasion and education, washing hands and bathing, going to the front with light burden, and consolidation against the enemy" were carried out in various places and over 95 percent of the cadres consolidated. The situation was encouraging. Yet in actual work, there still exist several problems. In some places, some cadres leading the Movement still have only one-sided understanding and methods. When the masses have not yet been mobilized and the struggle against capitalist and feudalist influences has not yet been launched, we are apt to ignore the seriousness of problems among basic-level cadres, and not be stern enough in the education and criticism of cadres who have committed mistakes. A sentiment of leniency and perfunctoriness prevails. When the lid of class struggle has completely been lifted and the masses have been fully mobilized, there may appear deviation which includes failure to distinguish the conflict between the enemy and ourselves and the internal conflict of the people, exaggeration of the enemy's strength, and forming a bad opinion of basic-level cadres and even regarding them as the major targets for our blows. Such deviations, especially the latter, are quite harmful and should be remedied and prevented.

Experiences gained in spot-testing at various places have proved that to consolidate over 95 percent of the cadres is a prerequisite to the consolidation of over 95 percent of the masses. When the question of the cadres is properly handled, the question of consolidating the masses will also be solved more easily. In actuality, the process of educating the cadres is also the process of educating the masses. When the work of educating the cadres is well done— when they are made to stand firm on their standpoint, make clear class lines, examine their mistakes and correct their manner—they will have set good examples for the self-education of the masses.

For the consolidation of over 95 percent of the cadres, we must see clearly the following important questions and should adopt correct measures to solve them:

1) Our view on the vast number of basic-level cadres should be thoroughly, not fragmentally, analysed. Among basic-level rural cadres, many have committed big or small mistakes. In some cases, the mistakes are comparatively more serious. In addition, a few landlords, rich peasants, counter-revolutionaries and undesirable elements have sneaked into the cadres' rank. This is one aspect of the situation. But, what is more important is that we should see that the great majority of basic-level rural cadres are good, and can stand firm on the road of socialism. In the process of positive participation in the class and production struggles, their defects and mistakes can be gradually remedied, and their ideological consciousness heightened. Among them, some 70 or 80 percent were tenant, poor, or lower-middle peasants during the land reform period. The majority of them were also positive elements during the land reform and collectivization periods. During the land reform struggles, and during the process of completing the agricultural collectivization, and in leading the agricultural production, they have done quite a lot of work. What most of them have committed today are mostly limited to such common mistakes as excessive eating, excessive possessions, and petty theft. Only a small part of them have made serious mistakes. This is another aspect, the basic aspect. Having viewed the basic-level rural cadres in this light, we may go on to consolidate over 95 percent of the cadres. As for the remaining 5 percent who have committed serious mistakes, they should also be analyzed. According to investigations conducted at some places, degenerates beyond salvation, and landlords, rich peasants, counter-revolutionaries and undesirable elements who have sneaked in, constitute only around one percent. The remaining 2, 3 or 4 percent have committed serious mistakes, and often they are connected with the class enemy. Some of them have already been won over by landlords and bourgeoisie, and the masses' indigation against them is great. Yet, they are still different from the class enemy. To deal with them, the directives of education, reform and consolidation should be adopted.

2) How to handle cadres who have committed mistakes? The general principle is: employ education and supplement it with punishment; distinguish the actual situation and deal with it accordingly; be strict in criticism and recovery

of misappropriated money and valuables, and lenient in handling by the organization; be strict to those who resist and lenient to those who admit their mistakes. In actual handling, we should grasp the following four points:

(a) Discriminate between policies. Aside from those listed above, we should pay special attention to the following discriminations: the discrimination between corruption and theft on the one hand, and excessive spending, excessive eating, unjustified possession, extravagance and waste on the other; discrimination between degeneration and ordinary mistakes concerning daily living.

(b) Do a good job in education. Concerning cadres who have committed mistakes, we should assume the attitude of treating the illness to save the man, to enthusiastically educate them and help them see and remedy their mistakes. Even toward degenerated cadres, we should adopt the attitude of doing our utmost to help them and, after criticisms and struggles, win over and remold those who can be won over and remolded. Many of our basic-level cadres suffered and were suppressed in the old society; to lead them to remember the old society and compare it with the new society is an easy way to raise their class consciousness. This is a very good method of education and has been proved successful in spot-testings at many places. It may be widely adopted in various places.

(c) Do a good job in financial reimbursement and compensation. Money and valuables obtained through corruption or theft, regardless of their quantities, must be reimbursed or compensated in full. As for those who engage in speculation and profiteering, they should be ordered to pay retrospective taxes, or fined, or turn in all of their illegal gains in accordance with the law and our policies. In short, those who have committed such mistakes should not be allowed to make financial gains, so that they learn a lesson and not repeat such mistakes. However, the calculation should be practical and the reimbursement, retrospective tax payment, and fine should be reasonable. These must be both satisfactory to the masses and acceptable to the wrong-doers. The period for calculating the reimbursement and compensation should not be too long. Except for gang leaders of corrupting, stealing, speculating, profiteering groups or repeated offenders, the period for calculating the reimbursement and compensation may begin from the time when the first revised draft of the 60 Articles was passed down to the villages, that is the latter half of 1961. If the valuables gained through corruption and theft are retrievable, they should be retrieved; if not, they may be paid for at prices fixed by the state or at the current market prices. If the offender cannot afford to pay all at once, he may pay by installment.

If those who have committed corruption, theft, speculation or profiteering have confessed and made reimbursement or compensation, they may be excused from the charges of being corrupt elements if the indignation of the people is not too serious. Yet serious offenders should be assigned other work and no longer permitted to continue as responsible cadres or in charge of money or valuables.

The cadres' mistakes of excessive eating and unjustified possession should all be severely criticized. In cases of large-scale or serious excessive eating and unjustified possession, the principle is that reimbursement and compensation should be effected. If the offender cannot afford to reimburse or compensate for all at once, he may do so by installments. If he has done a good job in self-examination and self-criticism, the amount of reimbursement or compensation may be duly cut down, upon agreement of the masses. In cases of ordinary excessive eating or unjustified possession, if the self-criticism is satisfactory and the masses agree, the offender may be excused from making reimbursement or compensation. When investigating excessive eating and unjustified possession, we should not go too far back in calculation. Generally it should begin from 1962.

(d) Do a good job in organizational management. In carrying out the job of management, the organization should be lenient. An offender who confesses on his own accord, does a satisfactory job in self-criticism, reimbursement and compensation, and shows determination of quitting wrong doings, may be handled with leniency or excused. In cases of serious offense, or unsatisfactory confession, reimbursement or compensation, and when the masses consider punishment necessary, then disciplinary action should be taken. The punishment should be appropriate. The offender should be given whatever punishment he deserves. The scope of punishment should be strictly controlled. Except for degenerated elements who are beyond salvation or former landlords, rich peasants, counter-revolutionaries or undesirable elements who have smuggled into the cadres' ranks (such persons should be purged completely), it is probably proper that the total number of cadres receiving punishment be fixed within two per cent, with hsien as the unit. The percentages of punished cadres in different places should be fixed by provincial, municipal and autonomous region Party committees, on the basis of actual circumstances.

To sum up, wrong-doing cadres should be handled with seriousness and caution. Data collected during the Movement should be double-checked and confirmed and 100 percent sure. Cadres should be dealt with after careful analyses and studies are made, and the nature of the problem and the seriousness of the case ascertained. Questions which cannot be clarified for the time being should be listed as special cases and be handled only after a clear investigation. Any problem in which it cannot be readily decided whether it is a contradiction between enemies and ourselves or an internal contradiction of the people, should first be handled as an internal contradiction of the people. Except for individual cases or cases that cannot be put off, all cases should be handled at the latter stage of the Movement, when the leadership and the masses have comparatively cooled off.

3) In this Socialist Education Movement, we should not only oppose bad men and bad deeds, but should also honor good men and good deeds. We should honor those cadres who are firm in their stand, positive in carrying out their work, enthusiastic about the collective, fair-minded in management, abiding by the system and the laws, hardworking, thrifty, active in collective labor, and liked by the masses, so as to set a good example for the vast cadres to follow.

4) The question of how to deal with cadres with the background of upper-middle peasants should be handled under the prerequisite that cadres with the background of poor and lower-middle peasants must constitute the majority in leading organizations. It should be handled with care, in accordance with actual circumstances. As for cadres with the background of new upper-middle peasants, as long as they resolutely carry out the Party's policies and are determined to walk the road of socialism together with the poor and lower-middle peasants, continued confidence should be placed upon them, and their leadership should remain unchanged. In cases where they discriminate against, or try to shove away poor and lower-middle peasants politically or economically, or when they commit more serious mistakes and the masses have lost confidence in them, proper measures may be adopted to make adjustments. In general, old upper-middle peasants are not fit to serve as leading func-

tionaries of basic organizations. However, some individuals among them, after long-term education by the Party, have comparatively higher socialist consciousness, stand firmly on the road of socialism, are fair-minded, capable, supported by the masses, and show good performance in many respects. They may also be permitted to continue their leading positions in the basic organizations.

Party members with the background of old upper-middle peasants should be judged by the standard required of the Party member. Whether they can serve as leading functionaries of basic organizations should not be based on their background, but on their "merits" and "ability."

5) Whether children of landlords and rich peasants, or those married to children of landlords and rich peasants may serve as basic cadres.

Sons and daughters of landlords and rich peasants, without exception, should be barred from positions as leading cadres of local basic units. Generally they are also unfit to take such important positions as accountant, work point recorder, and security officer. Yet some young students, workers returning to their native places, and demobilized servicemen, who are from landlords' or rich peasants' families, and who have undergone long inspection and proved good, may be assigned proper work according to actual needs (including social work). They should be educated and reformed on the job.

Whether Party members and cadres married to children of landlords and rich peasants can still remain Party members and cadres should mainly be based upon their own performance. The question should not be handled simply on the basis that they are married to offspring of landlords and rich peasants. Education of this element of Party members and cadres should be stepped up, to make them heighten their consciousness, draw clear political lines, be firm on class stand, and educate their spouses instead of being influenced by their spouses. As for those married to landlords or rich peasants, the case is of course completely different. Generally, they should not be allowed to be Party members or cadres.

VII. Concerning Cadre Participation In Collective Production Labor

The mobilization and organization of cadres for participation in collective production labor is one of the important programs of the Socialist Education Movement. In some regions where the Movement has not yet been launched, propaganda work and promotion of this program has already been carried out. At present, the situation of cadre non-participation in labor has improved in many places. But, in order to solve the problem completely, to make rural cadres of the whole country take part in collective labor seriously within three years, and consolidate the situation in a long-term manner, much work has yet to be done and many ideological and practical problems must first be solved.

At present, some cadres still do not understand the great revolutionary significance of participation in collective labor. The problem of their attitude of shirking and looking down upon labor has not yet been satisfactorily solved. In some leading organizations, especially in those at the hsien or commune levels, the bureaucratic leading manner has not yet been completely remedied. The situation of too many reports and forms still exists. In other places, inadequate attention is paid to actual difficulties resulting from cadres' participation in labor. All these have affected the firm establishment of the system of cadre participation in collective labor.

To solve such problems, three things must be stressed. They are: propaganda, the establishment of systems, and the improvement of leadership in leading organizations.

We must go a step further to heighten all cadres' understanding of the great revolutionary significance of participation in labor. The influence of a centuries-old concept of exploiting and despising labor is not easily wiped out. We should continue our propaganda and education for the basic-level cadres and organize them for serious and penetrating study of the Central Committee's documents concerning cadre participation in labor. Taking consideration of their ideological status, we should substantially solve their problems, so as to heighten their understanding of participation in collective labor, make them more conscious of it, and make them voluntarily participate in collective labor.

To regularize the participation in labor by cadres of production brigades and teams, a set of practical and applicable rules and working systems must be mapped out. These include fixing the number of days for their basic labor each year, setting up a standard for the cadres' extra allowance, and reasonable arrangement of work and labor.

In each brigade and team, the number of working days for each cadre and the number of subsidized work points to be allowed should all be fixed after they are discussed and agreed upon by commune members and the masses. The total number of subsidized work points for cadres of brigades and teams must be limited to two percent of the total points of the brigade or team.

The improvement of leadership in leading organizations at various levels, mainly at the hsien and commune levels, is an important guarantee for basic-level cadres' participation in labor. Cadres at the hsien and commune levels should, in accordance with the Central Committee's instructions of 1957 concerning cadres' participation in labor, devote a certain amount of time each year to reach the low strata of the society and labor with commune members in production teams. Participation of leading hsien and commune-level cadres in rural collective labor has a significant bearing on their understanding of the actual situation, their relations with the masses, and improvement of their working attitude. The examples set personally by the leading cadres will undoubtedly serve to inspire the vast number of basic-level cadres to action.

The Central Committee has repeatedly given instructions and orders that various business departments of the Central Government and leading organizations of various provinces, districts, hsien and communes simplify their meetings, and exercise strict control over statistical reports and forms. Yet, up to the present, these problems still are not satisfactorily solved in certain departments and places. This situation must immediately be remedied.

Leading organizations at the hsien and commune levels must strictly follow the stipulations of the 60 Articles—that excessive telephone conferences should be avoided and basic-level cadres not be summoned willy-nilly to meetings. Any conference that is not absolutely necessary, should be strictly avoided; any meeting that can be called at the low level should not involve the higher level; any meetings that can be merged should not be held separately; any discussion that can be split into several meetings should not be held in one meeting; any meeting that can wait until the idle farming season should not be held during the busy season. The summoning of commune-level cadres for meetings by business departments at the hsien level must first be approved by the hsien committee. Any meeting of brigade and team-level cadres called by the commune that lasts for two days or longer must be approved by the hsien committee.

Statistical forms should be issued uniformly and only by the hsien statistics department in accordance with stipulations of higher levels. Other organizations are not allowed to issue their own forms. The hsien statistics department must improve the current use of forms on the basis of the Statistics Bureau's announcement of April 15, 1963. Forms that should be kept should be listed and passed down to the people's commune. Any form not listed should not be used any longer. Committees at the provincial or district level should assign a secretary to make checks every six months on the matters of simplifying meetings and forms in the district. Personnel in charge of Party affairs of the Central Government business departments should also make checks every six months on the simplification of meetings and forms in that department, so as to cut down to a minimum the number of meetings and statistical forms.

VIII. Rectifying the Basic Party Organization in Rural Villages in Coordination with the Socialist Education Movement

The current Socialist Education Movement is, in fact, also a Party reform movement of mass nature. Experiences gained from spot-testings at various places prove that in places where intra-Party problems are serious, the relations between the Party and the masses are also strained and the class enemies active. Without rectifying the Party organizations, the Socialist Education Movement cannot be carried out smoothly. Experience also proves that this Movement not only gives each Party member a good education and training, but it also serves as a good test for each Party member. All these experiences indicate that it is both necessary and possible to rectify basic-level rural organizations.

Leading organizations at the provincial, regional and hsien levels, when making arrangements for the Socialist Education Movement, should emphasize Party rectification and strengthen their leadership in the work. When organizing the work teams, cadres with Party work experiences should be recruited to participate. The working team training program should include rectification of the Party.

Party reform in the villages is being carried out in close coordination with the Socialist Education Movement. The whole process of the Socialist Education Movement is the reform of the Party's basic level organizations. After going through this Socialist Education Movement, the Party's basic level organizations in rural villages should be made to meet the following requirements:

1) All Party members must go through an intensive class education and socialist education. They must judge themselves by the required standard of a Party member, and make criticisms and self-criticisms.

2) Problems within Party organizations should be thoroughly exposed. An examination of Party members' social stand, class stand, political background, ideological attitude, and work performance should be carried out.

3) Degenerated elements and landlords, rich peasants, counter-revolutionaries and undesirable elements who have sneaked into the Party should be completely purged.

4) Party members who have committed serious or comparatively serious mistakes and failed to repent after repeated persuasions should be properly dealt with.

5) Party members and cadres, especially Party branch secretaries, should be so educated that they will serve as examples of active participation in collective labor.

6) The leading nuclei of the Party's basic-level organizations should be reinforced and strengthened.

7) Routine work and organizational life of the Party's basic-level organizations should be set up and strengthened.

When the above-mentioned demands are fulfilled, the Party's basic organizations in rural villages can be said to have been fundamentally rectified.

"Follow the policy of learning from past experiences and applying them to future undertakings, and of healing people of their political ills and saving them, in order to achieve the twin goals of ideological clarification and unity of the comrades." The principle concerning the intra-Party struggle as laid down by Comrade Mao Tse-tung should be the fundamental principle to be followed in carrying out the Party rectification work in rural villages. To rectify the Party's basic-level organizations in rural villages, the method of combining intra-Party criticisms should be adopted. Meetings should first be convened within the Party; and subsequently Party meetings, participated in by positive elements from the poor and lower-middle peasants, should be held. Criticisms and self-criticisms should be carried out at these meetings. Party members who have committed mistakes should be handled in the latter part of the Movement. The punishment of Party members should be in accordance with the Party Constitution. The defendants should be allowed to explain and defend themselves, and all punishment should go through the proper procedure of approval by higher levels. For some chronically retarded and backward Party members, repeated education should be carried out. Proper handling shall only be after they are given ample time to learn and think it over. Some cases may wait for the registration of Party members.

It has not yet been decided whether or not to carry out the work of a new registration of Party members during this Movement. Experiments may be made in various places. They may either concentrate on the rectifying of Party basic-level organizations, while putting off the registration of Party members; or they may start the registration immediately on the basis of the Socialist Education Movement and the Party rectification. This matter may be decided after experiences are gained in spot testings.

IX. HANDLING OF LANDLORDS, RICH PEASANTS, COUNTER-REVOLUTIONARIES AND UNDESIRABLE ELEMENTS

During the Socialist Education Movement, the problems of landlords, rich peasants, counter-revolutionaries and various kinds of undesirable elements must be correctly handled. Our policy is resolutely to defeat the capitalist and feudalist forces in their attacks, to raise considerably through struggles the class consciousness of the vast number of peasants, especially the poor and lower-middle peasants, and to direct our blows accurately at landlords, rich peasants, counter-revolutionaries and undesirable elements engaged in serious sabotaging activities without, however, enlarging the scope of our attack.

To deal with the four elements engaged in activities of restoration and obstruction exposed during the Movement, we should mobilize the masses to carry out education and struggle in order to suppress them. After the struggle, these elements are to be put under the supervision of the masses, and, through the power of the masses, subjected to dictatorial treatment with a view to making the great majority of them "new men." Those who have committed violence in revenge, killing, pillaging, arson, and poisoning and have thus aroused great indignation of the people should be arrested and punished according to law immediately. Other "four elements" engaged in obstructive activities should be dealt with by adopting the basic principle of "killing none and arresting few (under 5 percent)." The few "four elements" engaged in obstructive activities who warrant immediate arrest should also first be put to a process of struggle conducted among the masses, so as to expose the enemy and educate the masses. At an opportune time, they are to be taken into custody according to law after due examination and authorization. The arrest of an offender should be strictly carried out under two conditions: first, the crime is serious, the evidence is clear and the offender shows no repentance; and second, the majority of the masses demand the arrest. By observing these two conditions, we cannot make mistakes in the arrest of offenders.

The reason why we should adopt the policy of "killing none and arresting few" (under 5 percent) in dealing with "four elements" engaged in obstructive activities is that by experience we know how to use the power of the masses against these elements; and, to subject them to supervision, struggle and education suits the people's interests better than to arrest and kill them. The reasons are: first, the great majority of them can be reformed to become good elements by the awakened masses through correct methods; second, they are part of the productive labor force of the society; and third, it would be advantageous to their sons and daughters.

Within a province or a special district, there will certainly be some elements who have committed serious crimes and refuse to repent and whose arrests are demanded by the majority of the masses. There will also be some individuals whose executions are demanded by the masses. These are altogether necessary.

The death sentence must first be approved by the Central Committee, in strict accordance with the past stipulations.

All illegal gains of landlords or rich peasants who have committed embezzlement, speculation, or theft should be handled sternly. Those who have speculated and profiteered should be ordered to pay retrospective tax, fines, or have their gains confiscated; those who have stolen should be ordered to return the valuables; those who have made gains by false accounting should return the whole sum involved. In short, the handling of financial matters must be strict, and the payments should be practical and based on facts.

In this Movement, the masses should be mobilized to carry out a general scrutiny and rating of the four elements, so as to heighten the regular supervision and reform of them. Those four elements against whom charges have been removed but who have again engaged in destructive activities and consequently should again be placed on the list, may be black-listed again upon approval of the hsien people's council; those four elements who have shown truly good work performance may be removed from the black list upon approval of the hsien people's council. At present in some rural villages, there is some confusion as to the targets for dictatorial treatment. For example, some landlords, rich peasants, counter-revolutionaries, undesirable elements and rightist elements evade the people's supervision by going from place to place, or by leaving the rural villages for cities. In this Movement, a clarification of the targets for dictatorial treatment should be carried out.

During the land reform, in some places some landlords and rich peasants escaped [being charged as rightists]. This situation varies with the place. In some places, the left-out landlords and rich peasants number more, in some places less, in some places none at all. Of the whole, the number should not be big. Therefore, in this Movement, it is not necessary to carry out a general work of investigation of left-out landlords and rich peasants. Yet, landlords and rich peasants who have been left out of the black list and who engage in destructive activities must be picked out and labelled "landlords" and "rich peasants," upon approval of the hsien people's council.

Our spot-testings show that during the past two years, due to various reasons, the economic life of quite a few families of landlords and rich peasants appeared much better off than the families of poor and lower-middle peasants. This tendency calls for our attention. From now on, in addition to strictly prohibiting them from engaging in illegal activities, we should fix the number of basic laboring days per month for each of them and fix their responsibilities in the civilian construction and labor program. Since their children do not join the army or the militia training, and they themselves seldom participate in meetings or other social activities, they should undertake a reasonably bigger portion of volunteer labor. Of course, the legal income they gain from labor should be protected. In the distribution of profits, they should receive the same reward for doing the same work. Otherwise, it would be harmful to both the production and to the work of reforming them.

X. CORRECT HANDLING OF THE QUESTION OF HOW TO DEAL WITH SONS AND DAUGHTERS OF LANDLORDS AND RICH PEASANTS

Offspring of former landlords and rich peasants constitute around 10 percent of the rural youths. General speaking, at present their political attitude and ideological condition can be described as "small at the two ends and big in the middle." This means that one minority of them, on account of deep family influence or keen desire for vengeance for the killing done on their kinfolk, are harboring intense class hatred toward the Party and the people, carry out class revenge and participate in the feudalist restoration and counter-revolutionary activities. Another minority of them are less influenced by family and seek political improvement, lean toward laboring people, and are willing to serve socialism. The great majority of them cannot draw a clear line between themselves and their families, have no feeling for the laboring people, and rate only fair in their political consciousness. These people are standing at a cross-roads and constitute the main targets in the fight between us and our class enemy in winning the youths. We should strengthen our work of educating and remolding them, encouraging them to revolt against their original classes, and to walk on the road of socialism. In the Socialist Education Movement, the consolidation of over 95 percent of the masses should include the majority of the sons and daughters of landlords and rich peasants, that is, those that can be won over.

In dealing with sons and daughters of landlords and rich peasants, two tendencies should be prevented and corrected. One is the lack of class viewpoint and class vigilance and the failure to carry out necessary struggle against reactionary remarks and acts of offspring of landlords and rich peasants. The other is to treat children of landlords and rich peasants in the same way as we do their parents—indiscriminately expelling them from the commune's membership; excluding them from any social work; and, in the cases of some members of the Young Communist League who return from urban factories and schools to participate in agricultural production in native villages, ignoring their organizational ties or refusing to let them attend the League's meetings. In some places, the League has even expelled its members who are from landlord and rich peasant families. Also, such members have been expelled from the Young Pioneers.

These two practices are all wrong, not serving the Party's interest.

Children of landlords and rich peasants, brought up in families of the exploiting class and receiving the influence of the exploiting class to various extents, are different from the children of the laboring people, especially those of poor and lower-middle peasants. However, the majority of the children of landlords and rich peasants are comparatively young, never directly participated in exploitation, are not exploiting elements, and should not be treated similarly as landlords and rich peasants. Sons and daughters of landlords and rich peasants who were not labelled as landlords or rich peasants during the land reform should not be branded as such now. Except for a few of them who are persistent in their reactionary stand, or who have been punished by law for committing crimes, they should be accepted as members of the communes, on the basis of their performance and upon approval of other commune members. When the "four elements" are summoned for meetings, their sons and daughters should not be called to attend the meetings or asked to attend in their places.

In this Socialist Education Movement, the work of educating and remolding the sons and daughters of landlords and rich peasants should be strengthened. They may be recruited to take part in mass rallies to receive education; they may also be summoned to attend meetings in which old poor and lower-middle peasants expose to them the history of exploitation by their families and the crimes of their parents, thus carrying out class education and heightening their understanding. For the relatively few landlords' or rich peasants' sons and daughters who have engaged in reactionary and destructive activities, necessary struggles and proper handling should be made. If their cases are serious, they should be punished according to law.

At some places, after the Socialist Education Movement is launched, restrictions are imposed on the marriages between Party members, League members, young poor, lower-middle peasants and sons and daughters of landlords and rich peasants. The marriages are forbidden. Those already married are considered as having lost their class stand, and in some cases they are even put under the discipline of the organization. Such are not proper measures. To treat this problem, we should educate young poor and lower-middle peasants, especially Party and League members among them, to teach them to heighten vigilance, to guard against falling into traps of the class enemy. Those who are already married should be taught to draw a clear political line, to be firm on class stand, and not to be affected by their spouses' bad influences. Yet, their marriages should not be restricted by any regulations.

Sons and daughters of landlords and rich peasants returning from urban factories and schools to participate in agricultural production in the villages should be welcomed. They should be consolidated and educated and their labor and work reasonably arranged, so as to utilize their functions well. As for those who are from families of landlords and rich peasants but who were directly brought up by revolutionary cadres or revolutionary soldiers, their family backgrounds should be those of revolutionary cadres or soldiers, and they should not be treated as sons and daughters of landlords or rich peasants.

APPENDIX D*

ORGANIZATIONAL RULES OF POOR AND LOWER-MIDDLE PEASANT ASSOCIATIONS (DRAFT)†

June, 1964

During the entire historical period of the transition from capitalism to communism, there continue to exist classes and class struggle; there exists struggle between the two roads of socialism and capitalism; and there exists the danger of a capitalist restoration. This class struggle, at certain times and under certain conditions, is acutely and severely manifested. The Chinese Communist Party, in its historical task of leading the entire nation and the entire people to complete the socialist revolution and socialist construction, still must resolve the basic question of on whom to rely and with whom to unite.

At the time of land reform, hired laborers, poor peasants, and lower-middle peasants comprised 60 to 70 percent of the rural population. They were the propertyless and the semi-propertyless. Except for the relatively few among them who rose to be new upper-middle peasants after land reform, they are the most active supporters of the socialist road and of collective production; they are the firm pillar of the dictatorship of the proletariat in the countryside; and they are the force which the party relies on in its rural work. To rely on the poor and lower-middle peasants and to unite with the other middle peasants is the class line which the Chinese Communist Party must implement in the rural areas over a long period of time.

In order to guarantee the thorough execution of this class line and to see to it that the poor and lower-middle peasants, during the struggle to consolidate the proletarian dictatorship, to consolidate the collective economy, and to develop agricultural production, are able to fully develop their function, on the basis of a call by the party Central Committee and Chairman Mao, there were established organizations of poor and lower-middle peasants throughout the whole countryside. From the Central Committee to the various local levels, there have been established leading organs for these organizations.

Poor and lower-middle peasant associations are led by the Chinese Communist Party. The various levels of party organization—especially the basic-level party organizations in the rural areas—must actively lead and support the work of the poor and lower-middle peasant associations, and must enable them to become a powerful arm of the party and a strong organization which unites the party with the laboring people in the whole countryside; moreover, through this organization, [we must] strengthen the education of the poor and lower-middle peasants and unceasingly raise their class consciousness; [we must] understand the aspirations and demands of the poor and lower-middle peasants and protect their interests.

ARTICLE I:

The poor and lower-middle peasant associations are voluntarily organized by the poor and lower-middle peasants under the leadership of the Chinese

---

* Acknowledgment is made of a translation in *Issues & Studies,* Institute of International Relations, Taipei, Vol. III, No. 11 (August 1967) pp. 44–51. This translation has been checked against the Chinese text and some editorial revisions made by the authors and the staff of the Center for Chinese Studies.

† *Chung-hua jen-min kung-ho-kuo p'in-nung hsia-chung-nung hsieh-hui tsu-chih t'iao-li (ts'ao-an)*

Communist Party, and are a class organization of a revolutionary mass nature.
ARTICLE II:

The basic tasks of the poor and lower-middle peasant associations are:

1) To respond actively to the call of the party and Chairman Mao to be exemplary in complying with and executing the policies and commands of the party and state, and to persist in the direction of socialism.

2) To carry on resolute struggle with the forces of capitalism and feudalism [in order to] guard against a restoration by the overthrown exploiting classes.

3) To unite with the middle peasants and with all those in the rural areas who can be united with, and together with them to take the socialist road.

4) To assist and supervise the various level organizations and cadres in the rural peoples communes to do a good job of managing the collective economy.

5) To actively develop the cadre function [ku-kan tso-yung] in production, so as to develop collective production.

6) With respect to the poor and lower-middle peasants and the other peasant masses, to carry out class education and socialist education, and to raise their political consciousness.
ARTICLE III:

All members of the rural peoples communes who are poor and lower-middle peasants regardless of nationality or sex, after they have submitted their applications, after having had their cases discussed at a meeting of the full membership of the peasant association within the production team, and after the peasant association committee of the production team has given its approval, may become members of the association.

Among the poor and lower-middle peasants, those people who have had serious questions concerning their political history; those people who have been in league with landlords, rich peasants, counter-revolutionaries, or bad elements; those people who have committed serious acts of corruption or theft or who have been opportunistic in their actions; and those people whose actions have severely undermined the interests of the collective economy or who have committed other serious mistakes—all these people, with the exception of those who have thoroughly, freely, and without reservation confessed their personal history; or who, despite having economic problems, have made indemnities; and who have undergone a long period of examination to prove whether they have truly corrected their mistakes—are absolutely not permitted to enter the poor and lower-middle peasant associations.
ARTICLE IV:

Within the organization of the poor and lower-middle peasant association, all association members have the right to elect and the right to be elected; all have the right to express their opinions on the subject of the work of the association; all have the right to criticize the shortcomings or mistakes of any leading member of the association. If, due to their criticism of the work of the commune or of the production team, or because of their criticism of cadres, they should be attacked as a means of gaining revenge, they have the right to demand that the association support them.

Members of the poor and lower-middle peasant association all must implement the resolutions of the association, and must actively complete the work assignments given them by the association. They must all actively participate in the work of supervising and reforming landlords, rich peasants, counter-revolutionaries and bad elements, and must struggle against all bad people and bad things. They must all perform the function of taking the lead and serving as model workers in supporting and consolidating the collective economy, and in developing agricultural production.

If members of the poor and lower-middle peasant association have committed mistakes, the association should, at a suitable time and place, carry out criticism and education, and help them to reform. If the mistakes are especially serious, and repeated attempts at reform have been unsuccessful, such cases may be discussed at a meeting of the full membership of the association within the production team, and after the association committee of the production team has given its approval, these people may be expelled from the peasant association. If those people who have thus been expelled from the association are unwilling to abide by this decision, their cases may be brought before a higher-level organization of the peasant association.

ARTICLE V:

The leading national organ of the poor and lower-middle peasant associations is the All-China Poor and Lower-Middle Peasant Association.

The highest authoritative organ of the poor and lower-middle peasant associations is the National Congress of Poor and Lower-Middle Peasants. The National Congress elects the Committee of the All-China Poor and Lower-Middle Peasant Association, which serves as its standing organ [ch'ang-she chi-kuan].

The Committee of the ACPLMPA elects one person to serve as chairman and a certain number of people to serve as vice-chairmen and standing committee members. Together they constitute a standing committee which gives unified leadership to the work of the peasant associations throughout the whole country.

ARTICLE VI:

The various local level organizations of the poor and lower-middle peasant associations are the provincial, municipal, autonomous regional, and hsien poor and lower-middle peasant associations. The authoritative organs of the peasant associations at each geographical organizational level are the provincial, municipal, autonomous regional, and hsien Poor and Lower-Middle Peasant Congresses. The Congress at each level elects its own committee, which serves as its standing organ.

The committee of the peasant association at each level elects one person to serve as chairman and a certain number of people to serve as vice-chairmen and standing committee members; these people constitute the standing committee, which gives unified leadership to the work of the peasant associations within its particular geographical jurisdiction.

At the level of special district, and in districts below the hsien level, on the basis of existing conditions, there may be established poor and lower-middle peasant association work committees to serve as representative organs of the provincial, autonomous regional, and hsien peasant association committees.

ARTICLE VII:

The basic-level organizations of the poor and lower-middle peasant associations are the peasant associations at various levels within the rural peoples commune.

The authoritative organs of the commune, production brigade, and production team-level peasant associations are the peasant association members' congresses at each level, or an assembly of the peasant association membership. They each elect a chairman, one or two vice-chairmen, and a certain number of committee members, who then constitute the peasant association committee, which is responsible for day-to-day work.

In relatively large production teams, on the basis of existing conditions, these may be broken down into several poor and lower-middle peasant small groups. In those production teams of an excessively small scale, and in those teams where the number of poor and lower-middle peasants is excessively small, on the basis of existing conditions, it may suffice to simply organize poor and lower-middle peasant small groups, rather than setting up a peasant association; it is also possible to join together members from several different teams to organize a peasant association or a small group. Poor and lower-middle peasant small groups each elect a group leader and one or two assistant group leaders, who are responsible for day-to-day work.

The terms of office for leading members at each level of the poor and lower-middle peasant organizations within the peoples commune is one year. They may be re-elected or re-appointed.

ARTICLE VIII:

Among the leading members of the peasant associations at each level within the peoples commune, it must be guaranteed that the old hired peasants and poor peasants constitute the absolute majority; there must also be a certain number of lower-middle peasants. Among [the leading members], there also ought to be a certain number of young people and women. In areas with mixed nationalities, there also ought to be a certain number of [leading] members from minority nationalities. The leading members of the peasant association organizations ought to be advanced elements who have a firm standpoint, who warmly love the collectivity, who labor actively, who handle their jobs equitably, and who receive the support of the masses.

The chairmen and group leaders at every level of poor and lower-middle peasant organizations within the peoples commune may not serve concurrently in any of the following positions: commune leader, production brigade leader, production team leader, accountant or payroll officer, guardian of valuables [pao-kuan yüan], or manager of communal or brigade-run enterprises and occupations.

The chairmen, group leaders, committee members, and representatives of poor and lower-middle peasant organizations in the production brigades and production teams must not become divorced from production and must not enjoy fixed work-point subsidies.

The chairmen, group leaders, committee members, and representatives of poor and lower-middle peasant organizations in the production brigades and production teams must all pay attention to developing the organizational function of the peasants association, and must all pay attention to developing the function of broadening the membership of the association. They must all be intimately linked with the masses of association members, and must understand the opinions and demands of peasant association members. All important questions should be dealt with by holding discussion meetings; the individual's opinion must never be allowed to be substituted for the organization's opinion.

ARTICLE IX:

The poor and lower-middle peasant organizations at each level within the peoples commune must all actively develop the function of being a support of the party, and must regularly, in the work of issuing reports to the commune party committee and to the brigade party branches, reflect the opinions of the poor and lower-middle peasants and other commune members; and, under the leadership of the party, they must actively popularize and implement the party's policies.

The commune party committee and brigade party branches ought to set a time for discussing the work of the poor and lower-middle peasant organizations, and should guide them in developing regular activities; they should also pay attention to cultivating a backbone force of cadres within the peasant organizations. All important matters of the commune and brigades, before being decided on by the party, should be talked over with the peasant organizations; after discussion and subsequent decision by the party, [the decision] should first be conveyed to and discussed within the peasant organizations. Party organizations at each level must regularly educate their own members and cadres to conscientiously implement the party's class line in the rural areas, and to consciously rely on the poor and lower-middle peasant organizations in carrying out all work.

ARTICLE X:

Poor and lower-middle peasant organizations at each level of the peoples commune should set a good example in carrying out the resolutions of the commune congresses and commune members assemblies [she-yüan tai-piao ta-hui, ho she-yüan ta-hui], and should take the lead in completing tasks assigned by these congresses and assemblies. Whenever the commune congress or commune members assembly calls a meeting to make a decision on an important question, all poor and lower-middle peasant organizations should, as their first order of business, hold discussion meetings for the purpose of introducing their own proposals.

ARTICLE XI:

Poor and lower-middle peasant organizations at each level of the peoples commune should actively assist and supervise the work of management committees. Management committees at each level, when deciding important questions, should first solicit the opinions of the poor and lower-middle peasant organization. Each peasant organization may send representatives to attend meetings of the management committee at its own level. Poor and lower-middle peasant organizations should actively support—and take the lead in implementing—all correct decisions of the management committees; but they must not do the latter's work for them.

If there should occur differences of opinion between the peasant organizations and the management committee over an important question, and if unanimity still cannot be achieved after mutual consultation, a meeting of the commune members assembly or the commune congress may be proposed in order to carry on discussion. If necessary, the opinion of a higher-level party organization or higher-level peasant association may be solicited.

ARTICLE XII:

Poor and lower-middle peasant organizations at each level of the peoples commune should assist and supervise the cadres at each level to correctly execute the policies of the party and state, to hold a firm class standpoint, to actively participate in collective labor, to reform their thought modes and working styles, to implement democratic commune management [min-chu pan-she], to foster a close relationship between cadres and the masses, and to do a good job of managing the collective economy.

Poor and lower-middle peasant organizations at each level of the peoples commune should actively support all correct opinions and measures of the cadres in their work at the communal, production brigade, and production team levels. With respect to those cadres whose standpoint is resolute, who are fair and just in the handling of their jobs, and who actively serve the people, [the peasant organizations] ought to propose to the party and government organs that these cadres be given publicity and encouragement. Toward those cadres who have shortcomings and who have committed mistakes, [the peasant organizations] ought to, whenever convenient, carry on criticism and exposure, and may present evidence and lodge a complaint with control organs [*chien-ch'a tsu-chih*] or higher-level party policy-making organs. No one will be permitted to obstruct, hinder, or interfere; even less will anyone be permitted to retaliate.

ARTICLE XIII:

Poor and lower-middle peasant organizations at each level of the peoples commune should treat the supervisory work of seeing that management committees and cadres at each level strictly implement the system of financial management and persist in diligently and frugally managing the commune as one of their own regular, important jobs. They must assist the management committees and control organs at each level in carrying out the annual or semi-annual work of cleaning up accounts, warehouses, properties, and work points. They must promptly criticize and expose such actions as eating too much or owning too much, extravagance and waste, nepotistic malpractices, corruption, theft, and destruction of public property; and when the circumstances surrounding such acts are serious, they should propose that the departments concerned handle these cases severely.

ARTICLE XIV:

Poor and lower-middle peasant organizations at each level of the peoples communes must regularly pay attention to preventing and checking the spread of spontaneous capitalistic tendencies, and must wage struggles against the forces of capitalism. With respect to such phenomena as undermining the interests of the state or of the collectivity and encroaching upon public property, paying undivided attention to developing the private economy, abandoning agriculture to go into private business, and speculating and profiteering, [the peasant organizations] must carry on discussion and study; they must also remonstrate with and criticize the people who commit these mistakes; and, where conditions are serious, they must promptly expose such acts and propose that the departments concerned handle these cases.

ARTICLE XV:

Poor and lower-middle peasant organizations at each level of the peoples commune must assist public security departments in strengthening the supervision and reformation of landlords, rich peasants, counter-revolutionaries and bad elements; they must treat this type of work as one of their own regular tasks. Peasant organizations at each level must constantly maintain their revolutionary vigilance; they must regularly comprehend and study the thought and activities of these four classes of bad elements, and must promptly report these conditions to the public safety departments; they must expose all illegal and destructive activities; and they must, in the process of productive labor, effectively strengthen the work of reforming these elements.

ARTICLE XVI:

Poor and lower-middle peasant organizations at each level of the peoples commune must rouse the broad masses of commune members to develop the spirit of bitter struggle, the spirit of enthusiastic emulation, and the spirit of self-strengthening; they must actively transform the face of nature and vigorously develop collective production. Peasant organizations at each level must educate their members to care about collective production, to love and protect public property, to be exemplary in complying with labor discipline, to guarantee the qualities of rural work [*nung-huo chih-liang*], to raise labor efficiency, and to develop the function of taking the lead in production; they must arouse and organize their members to actively participate in scientific experimentation in agriculture, to study advanced technology, and to strive to bring about the modernization of agriculture.

100

ARTICLE XVII:

Poor and lower-middle peasant organizations at each level of the peoples commune should regularly be concerned about the lives of the poor and lower-middle peasants and other commune members who have encountered difficulties and should defend their right to participate in collective labor. They should promptly bring the opinions and demands of commune members to the attention of the management committees, and should assist and push forward the management committees in helping to solve the difficulties encountered by commune members in everyday life and in production. On the question of distributing state relief funds and livelihood loans [*sheng-huo tai-k'uan*], and in the utilization of public welfare reserves, before a decision can be made by the management committee or by the commune congress or commune members assembly, all questions must first be discussed by the peasant organizations.

ARTICLE XVIII:

Poor and lower-middle peasant organizations at each level of the peoples commune must organize the peasant association members to study the works of Chairman Mao and the policies of the party Central Committee; they must teach their members to heed the words of the party Central Committee and Chairman Mao and to do their jobs in accordance with the directives of the party Central Committee and Chairman Mao.

[Peasant organizations] must regularly conduct class education and education in socialism, collectivism, patriotism, and internationalism for the benefit of all peasant association members; they must continuously raise the level of their class consciousness, socialist consciousness, and political consciousness. They must pay particular attention to teaching the rural youth and children to carry on and develop the revolutionary traditions of the proletariat, and to become good successors to the cause of socialist construction.

[Peasant organizations] must organize the members of the peasant associations to study cultural and scientific knowledge, to smash feudal superstitions, to transform backward customs and habits, and to advocate new, socialist customs and habits.

SOME CONCRETE POLICY FORMULATIONS OF THE CENTRAL COMMITTEE OF THE CHINESE COMMUNIST PARTY IN THE RURAL SOCIALIST EDUCATION MOVEMENT †

(Revised Draft, September 10, 1964)

The "Draft Resolution on Some Problems in Current Rural Work" issued by the Central Committee in May, 1963, is a great and basic document. It is an important document concerning the basic construction of our Party on the ideological, political, organizational and economic fronts.

The document dealt with ten problems, greatly augmenting the contents of the Socialist Education Movement which has been pushed in various rural villages since the tenth plenum of the eighth Central Committee.

Since the summer and fall of 1963, in accordance with the resolutions contained in this document, a widespread rural Socialist Education Movement has been launched in various places after several spot-testings. During the past year, experience gained from this Socialist Education Movement in various places has amply proved that Comrade Mao Tse-tung's analyses and instructions on such problems as classes, class contradiction, and class struggle in a socialist society have great revolutionary and historic significance. It has also fully proved that this Movement, launched in accordance with Comrade Mao's instructions, has long range and far reaching significance in repulsing the fanatic offensive of the imperialist and feudalist forces, in consolidating the stand of rural socialism and proletarian dictatorship, in destroying the social basis from which revisionism stems, in consolidating collective economy, and in developing agricultural production. At the same time, it also has clearly demonstrated that this Movement is a large-scale mass movement more widespread, more complicated, and more meaningful than the land reform movement. Only by freely mobilizing the masses can this Movement achieve complete victory.

For implementing the draft resolution of the Central Committee one step further, and for solving some problems concerning concrete policies of the movement, the Central Committee in September 1963 promulgated "Some Concrete Policy Formulations of the Central Committee of the Chinese Communist Party in the Rural Socialist Education Movement (Draft)." Now, the Central Committee, with new experience, has made important revisions of the draft. The following is the revised formulation:

I. BASIC DIRECTIONS AND MAIN CONTENTS OF THE SOCIALIST EDUCATION MOVEMENT

[First paragraph is quotation from Mao Tse-tung: see Appendix C.]

In accordance with Comrade Mao Tse-tung's instructions, this Movement

---

*Acknowledgment is made of a translation in *Issues & Studies,* Institute of International Relations, Taipei, Vol. I, Nos. 10 and 11, July and August 1965 (pp. 1–12 and 27–43 respectively). This translation has been checked against the Chinese text and some editorial revisions made by the authors and the staff of the Center for Chinese Studies. Because this is a revision of the document which appears as Appendix C, duplicated material has been omitted. It is hoped that this will highlight the changes that have been made; but for continuity and coherence, the reader will have to refer to the similarly numbered sections of Appendix C.

† *Chung-kung chung-yang kuan-yü nung-ts'un she-hui chu-i chiao-yü yün-tung chung i-hsieh chü-t'i cheng-ts'e ti kuei-ting (hsiu-cheng ts'ao-an)*

should take class struggle as its principle and grasp five vital points. These are: struggle against the enemy, socialist education, organize the class forces of the poor and lower-middle peasants, the Four Cleans, and cadre participation in collective labor. The key and prerequisite for correctly launching and leading the Socialist Education Movement is to study the thought of Comrade Mao Tse-tung concerning such questions as classes, class contradictions, and class struggle in a socialist society; and then to understand clearly and remember these thoughts. Take class struggle as a principle; grasp the five vital points; give free rein to the masses; launch a mass Socialist Education Movement by stages and with leadership; first unite more than 95 percent of the masses; conscientiously resolve the problems of Four Uncleans among the cadres; move forward to unite more than 95 percent of the cadres; repulse the offensive of feudal and capitalist forces; elevate the socialist and class consciousness of cadres and masses; readjust the basic-level organizations in the villages; make further strides in strengthening the collective economy and in developing agricultural production—all these are basic directives for this Socialist Education Movement.

During this Movement, we must systematically carry out the following twelve items of work.

1) Convene cadre meetings of commune, brigade, and production team levels, with participation by representatives of poor and lower-middle peasants, to expound the policies of the Party. Those cadres who have committed mistakes should be brought voluntarily at these meetings to "wash their hands and bodies" and "dump their burdens."

2) Publicly read and explain among the masses the draft resolutions of the Central Committee and this draft formulation, thus transmitting the Party policies directly to the masses.

3) [See same numbered paragraph in Appendix C.]

4) With full mobilization of the masses and on the foundation of work to improve the ideology of the cadres, carry out the Four Cleans. Problems of retrieving misappropriated money from the cadres or making them repay what has been misused should be handled correctly.

5) Educate the masses in socialism, collectivism, patriotism, and internationalism. A clear line must be drawn between socialism and capitalism; and the problems of the relationship between public and private, and the struggle between socialism and capitalism, should be solved.

6) Clearly classify class backgrounds and establish class files.

[For sections 7 through 11 see same numbered paragraphs in Appendix C.]

12) Improve management and administration of production teams and map out production plans in accordance with the 60 Articles.

The 12 items of work listed above constitute the main contents of this Socialist Education Movement. They are inter-related and mutually supplementary and may be carried out simultaneously. We must see to it that they are carried out thoroughly, so that the Socialist Education Movement can be brought to a successful conclusion.

The whole work of this Socialist Education Movement can, generally speaking, be divided into two stages. In the first stage, the major work will be the solution of the problem of Four Uncleans among cadres, and the launching of struggle against the enemy. In the second stage, which is the period of organization and construction, the Party's basic organizations, the communes and brigade organizations, and the militia establishments will be readjusted. The two stages are closely related. While the first stage work programs are being carried out, preparations should also be made and foundations laid for the work of the second stage. What is especially important is that after good working teams have been established in rural villages, they should carefully and gradually recruit good and comparatively good members, cadres, and positive elements among the masses and work together with them. In other words, a new force should be built up during the movement.

Comrade Mao Tse-tung has repeatedly instructed us to carry out thoroughly the Socialist Education Movement. It will be probably five to six years, or even longer, before this Movement can be carried out in all rural villages. In this Movement, we must meet the demands of the Central Committee's draft resolution that "it should be implemented firmly and step by step; perfunctoriness must be strictly prohibited." From the leading levels of province, district, and hsien, down to the work teams and members of the teams, all must work hard to enable the Socialist Education Movement to achieve higher, or comparatively higher, qualitative and quantitative standards. Comrade Mao Tse-tung once said:

> What is the yardstick to measure the work of the Socialist Education Movement? First, we must see whether the poor and lower-middle peasants are really mobilized. Second, we must see whether the problem of Four Uncleans among cadres has been thoroughly solved. Third, whether the cadres have joined in the physical labor. Fourth, whether a good leading nucleus has been set up. Fifth, upon discovery of landlords, rich peasants, counter-revolutionaries and undesirable elements engaged in destructive activities, whether the contradiction has been passed up to the higher levels, or whether the masses have been aroused to carry out strict supervision and criticism and even appropriate struggle against these elements thus retaining them for on-the-spot reform. Sixth, we must see whether production has been increased or decreased.

These six conditions suggested by Comrade Mao Tse-tung may serve as the major yardstick for measuring the achievement of the Socialist Education Movement.

II. Several Problems Requiring Attention in Leading the Socialist Education Movement

The key to the questions of whether the Socialist Education Movement can be carried out smoothly, whether the masses can be fully mobilized, and whether the Party's policies can be correctly carried out during this Movement, lies in the leadership. Leading organizations at provincial, regional and hsien levels must pay close attention to the following points:

1) Lead the "hand-washing" and "bathing." Cadres of provincial, regional and hsien leading organizations, especially major leading cadres, must first of all "wash hands" and "take a bath." They must first correct their class stand and improve their thinking and work style before they can lead in the Socialist Education Movement. Otherwise, it will be impossible for them to do so. Some of the leading cadres cannot be said to be free from faults, yet they do not seriously examine and correct themselves. The masses have lost respect for them. When such cadres ask their subordinates to carry out the "Four Cleans," they cannot possibly expect good results. Therefore, all cadres at provincial, regional and hsien levels should first participate in the Five-Anti movement.

2) Personal squatting at points by leading personnel. Important leading personnel at the provincial, special district and hsien levels must personally squat at points in order to obtain experiences, set examples, and direct and

push forward the entire Movement. If the leading personnel do not act in this manner but instead rely on listening to reports and reading written materials for understanding the situation and directing the Movement, then they certainly will not be able to perform their work well and will commit mistakes. In squatting at points, they must truly squat at the lower levels. They must complete the work at a point from beginning to end, including organizing and training the work team, entering the villages to establish contacts and take root, mobilizing the masses and organizing the class ranks, and also including carrying out well the Four Cleans and the struggle with the enemy, readjusting organization, establishing and strengthening various systems, implementing the 60 Articles, and stimulating a high tide in production. Only by doing this directly from beginning to end can they gain complete experiences. They must squat in a production brigade and moreover use one or two production teams as key points in their own work, and personally participate in work. Only in this way can they have personal understanding of the true facts and genuine feeling, or gain direct experiences. Each leading official must at the minimum squat two times at a point in this manner; only then can he make comparisons and obtain correct, successful experiences. Personally squatting at points by leading personnel is an unusually important question. The current revolutionary struggle in the countryside is a new revolution, a revolution whose contents are very rich and which has many new special features. At present, the enemy's methods of opposing the proletarian dictatorship and socialism are becoming even more cunning. They associate with and corrupt cadres, implement peaceful transition, and establish a counter-revolutionary two-faced regime. They also utilize certain articles of our documents to carry out legal struggle against us. These are the main forms of the enemy's opposition to us. We are still very unfamiliar with class struggle under these new conditions and with this new revolution. If one does not personally go deeply into practice, one will not be able truly to understand this class struggle and this revolution, and naturally will not correctly lead them. Therefore, personal squatting at points by these comrades is a prerequisite to leading this great revolutionary movement well.

3) Organize staunch work teams. To launch the Socialist Education Movement at any point requires the sending of a work team from the higher level. The whole Movement should be led by the work team. The missions of the work team include: mobilization of the masses, execution of policies, completion of various items of work of the Socialist Education Movement. Each and every work team should be "led by politically strong and capable persons" in accordance with Comrade Mao Tse-tung's instructions. The work team must be high in quality and capability. Its members must be recruited through strict screening and examination. Anyone who is politically unreliable, who is seriously questionable in ideology and behavior, who showed serious mistakes during the Five-Anti period but has not undergone self-examination, should be excluded. All members of the work team must study seriously the Party's and Comrade Mao Tse-tung's instructions concerning the problems of socialist education, and understand and be well-versed in the Party's policies. The work team should possess the spirit of thorough revolution, maintain a work pattern, strictly follow the work discipline, so as to set a good example for the farming masses and rural cadres. Each work team should include several women cadres who can mobilize the women to the fullest extent. To achieve smooth development of the Socialist Education Movement, each province, municipality, or autonomous region should organize a number of specialized work teams consisting of a suitable number of members. These teams should

settle down at a place for a long period and concentrate on the Movement. After several rounds of such work, these work teams will become skilled teams, and from among the members we may gradually cultivate a backbone force to engage in socialist revolutionary work and rural work.

4) Boldly mobilize the masses. Among all work items of the Socialist Education Movement, mobilization of the masses should be put in the first place. It is the fundamental task in developing the Social Education Movement. Either in organizing the class ranks to carry out the Four Cleans, or in launching a struggle against the enemy, we should mobilize the masses to the fullest extent so as to make the Movement a truly self-awakening revolutionary struggle of the masses. The key to the mobilization of masses lies in the mobilization of poor and lower-middle peasants. Only when the poor and lower-middle peasants are mobilized and, around this axis, other laboring masses of the rural villages are also mobilized, plus careful ideological education of the cadres and a practical working attitude, can the various problems of the Movement be thoroughly solved, and over 95 percent of the masses and cadres truly consolidated.

Without the mobilization of the general masses, the work team concerns itself only with activity within the circle of basic-level cadres; it will be "much ado about nothing" for a few people. Thus the Movement will end in failure or reap very negligible results, and the consequences may be quite serious. All these are borne out in the experiences gained from the Movement work in various places during the past year.

Some of the comrades are hesitant in mobilizing the masses, having various kinds of concerns. Other cadres are opposed to the mobilization of the masses, using one thousand and one excuses. They are all very wrong. Only by thoroughly mobilizing the masses can this drive become a far-reaching revolutionary movement. All those who have a wavering attitude toward the Socialist Education Movement, first waver on the question of mobilizing the masses. All those who oppose the Socialist Education Movement, first oppose mobilizing of the masses. Education of the wavering ones should be intensified; they should be relieved of their anxieties and made firm. Those who oppose the Movement or obstruct the mobilization of the masses should be severely criticized. For more serious cases, necessary punishment should also be meted out. The Central Committee draft resolution and the present draft formulation both call for and support mass struggle; only by mobilizing the masses to the fullest extent can the various requirements contained in these two documents be met.

In this draft of policy formulations, concrete policies for various aspects of the Socialist Education Movement are set forth. This is necessary and is an important assurance for the smooth development and final success of this Movement. However, these policy decisions can be correctly and thoroughly implemented only after the masses are fully mobilized. We must not turn these indispensable, correct decisions into taboos obstructing the mobilization of the masses and binding our own hands and feet. This must be clearly understood by leading functionaries and members of working teams.

5) Correct treatment of the relationship between the [Socialist Education] Movement and production. The Movement and production should be closely coordinated. Stressing production while ignoring the Movement or vice versa, is wrong. At present, there generally exists among some of our cadres a situation in which the Movement and production are opposed.

They are afraid that when the Movement is pushed far and wide it may affect production. This is very wrong. Leading comrades at various levels and comrades of the work teams must all understand that class struggle and revolutionary movement are generative forces for developing production, and serve in the production struggle. Only after problems in the class struggle are solved, and the question of human relations is correctly handled, can we really utilize the people's positive spirit in production and make big headway in production. We should and must put the Socialist Education Movement in the first place. Of course, when we stress taking firm hold of the Movement, we should also pay close attention to productive work. Each work team should not only thoroughly carry out the Movement, but also lend a helping hand to the production brigade or team in solving pressing production problems, so as to achieve a truly good production result. All work arrangement and development should not interfere with the farming. During the Movement, attention should be paid at all times to the channeling of the masses' political enthusiasm and positiveness in labor to the consolidation of collective economy and the development of agricultural production.

6) Integration of point and plane. Socialist education work on the plane should be positively accomplished. Work on the point, which takes about six months to finish, should be done with utter care. Work on the plane, including the checking of the evil influences, mobilization of masses, preliminary regulation of the masses-cadres relationship, and dealing preliminary blows to the class enemy, requires only one or two months to do. The reason that point and plane should be connected is that this Socialist Education Movement is being developed from point to plane, and step by step. At a particular time, the majority of the communes and brigades are temporarily not systematically engaged in the Movement. Pushing the Movement on the points will certainly have a great impact on the plane. Also, we should continue to take hold of places where the Movement has already been systematically pushed, so as to consolidate these places. If we relax our efforts on the vast plane, serious losses will come as a result. Therefore, on the plane, aside from the assignment of special personnel to take charge and do routine work, the following items should also be carried out.

(a) With district or commune as a unit, convene three level or four level cadre meetings. All Party members and representatives of poor and lower-middle peasants should be called upon to participate, to study the draft resolutions of the Central Committee and the draft of these policy formulations, to understand the direction, policy and aim of this Movement, and to heighten consciousness and dispel anxieties. Later, cadres dispatched by the higher levels should combine with cadres of the communes and brigades to form work teams and to carry out widespread and far-reaching publicity among the masses, in order to wield influence.

(b) [See same numbered paragraph of Appendix C.]
(c) [See same numbered paragraph of Appendix C.]
(d) [See same numbered paragraph of Appendix C.]
(e) [See same numbered paragraph of Appendix C.]
(f) [Text follows same numbered paragraph of Appendix C but the following material is added at the end.] Socialist Education Movement on the plane should be held once every year, no matter whether the place has already undergone a systematic education movement or not.

III. CONSOLIDATE THE MORE THAN 95 PERCENT OF THE PEASANTS

The consolidation of over 95 percent of the peasants, as advocated by Comrade Mao Tse-tung, is a basic policy in pushing the Socialist Education Movement.

To truly consolidate over 95 percent of the peasant masses essentially depends on whether we have firmly and comprehensively implemented the Party's class line in the villages. Poor and lower-middle peasants, who constitute 60 or 70 percent of the rural population, are the staunchest supporters of the socialist line and the collective economy. To carry out the Socialist Education Movement, we must first mobilize fully the poor and lower-middle peasants, in order to use them as the basic force for mobilizing and consolidating other peasants. When our work among the poor and lower-middle peasants is satisfactorily completed, there will be firm assurance that consolidation of over 95 percent of the peasants will successfully be carried out.

One most important condition for successful consolidation of over 95 percent of the peasants is the complete solution of problems of the cadres, and the correction of the irregular relationships between some cadres and the masses. If cadres of a particular commune, production brigade, or production team show serious signs of Four Uncleans, have not returned or compensated for valuables they embezzled, do not participate in the collective labor, do not follow the class line, are not firm on the class stand, or are undemocratic in their attitude and behavior, the masses will have many complaints and be disgruntled. Thus, their political and collective production positiveness will not be utilized to the fullest extent. Under these circumstances, to try to firmly consolidate the vast masses will naturally be impossible. Therefore, in order to consolidate over 95 percent of the peasants, we must seriously and thoroughly solve the problems of the cadres, especially those who lead in the core of the basic-level organizations.

The Socialist Education Movement is a program of the self-education of the masses. Every member of the commune should undergo a far-reaching class education and socialist education. For heightening the peasants' consciousness so as to go a step further to strengthen the collective economy, it is very important seriously and properly to solve the problems concerning the relationship between public and private, as well as the struggle between socialist and capitalist lines in the Movement. In many places, this work has been well handled and has reaped satisfactory results. This is an important step in the consolidation of over 95 percent of the peasants. However, the process of this work should and must be coordinated with the cadres issue. In other words, to solve the problems concerning the relationship between the public and the private, and the struggle between the two lines among the masses, we must first satisfactorily solve the problems of the cadres. Here are some examples. In order to educate the masses in correct handling of the relations between the state, the collective body, and the individual, we must first educate the cadres to handle correctly the relations between the three. In order to educate, criticize and correct some people in the masses who undermine the collective economy, who eagerly develop "narrow freedom" and who do not positively participate in collective productive labor, we must first educate and criticize those cadres who have committed such mistakes and make them repent. In order to educate the masses to give up collective property and state-owned materials which they have appropriated, we must first educate the cadres to do so; similarly, in order to educate the masses to withdraw from the collective land they have occupied, we must first teach the cadres to do the same. In short, to educate the masses we must first educate the cadres; and to solve the problems of the masses we must first solve the problems of the cadres. Facts have proved that if some wrong-doing cadres, through education and with help from the masses, have examined their own mistakes, firmly taken a correct stand, drawn a clear political line, given back what they wrongly held and compensated for the loss, and improved their attitude, they will have set a good example for the self-education of the masses. Thus, some problems of the masses will be solved more easily.

In carrying out socialist education of the masses, our methods must be correct. We must adopt a policy of education by persuasion. When the peasants have shown defects and mistakes, we must apply the method of "unity-criticism-unity" to carry out the education with patience. We may also adopt such measures as "recollection" and "comparison," to enlighten them, improve their understanding, and make them repent of their own accord. To deal with them, no struggle rally, no false accusation, and especially no beatings are allowed.

To consolidate over 95 percent of the peasants, clear demarcation of policy lines is necessary in carrying out the concrete work of the Socialist Education Movement. We should distinguish between the class enemy who attempts to stage a comeback, and the backward elements who allow themselves to be utilized by the enemy out of temporary foolishness. We should distinguish between speculators and those who show more serious spontaneous capitalist tendency. We should distinguish between speculative activities and proper activities of marketing and trading. We should distinguish between the spontaneous force of capitalism and proper family sideline occupations of commune members. We should distinguish between high-interest exploitation loaning and mutual assistance and normal economic transactions among commune members. We should distinguish between corruption, larceny, and petty theft. We should distinguish between such acts as collecting money by utilizing feudal superstition, restoration of feudalist and family rule and carrying out counter-revolutionary activities on the one hand, and the backward customs and habits and common superstitious acts of the masses on the other. In handling these cases, we should adopt an attitude of practicality, make actual analyses, and take careful measures. We should deal with a problem as it is, without exaggerating or minimizing its importance. Otherwise, we will undermine the policy, harm the masses, and damage the Movement. All these measures concerning demarcation of policy lines are equally applicable to solving the problems of cadres. In fact, they must be applied first to solving the problems of cadres, because the problems involved in the demarcation of policy lines are mainly found among the cadres.

[Next to last paragraph duplicates third from last paragraph of Appendix C, Section III.]

[Last paragraph commences: "Dependents of officers and soldiers of the People's Liberation Army and public security forces mostly are poor and lower-middle peasants." (cf. opening sentence of next to last paragraph in Appendix C, Section III).]

[Final paragraph in Appendix C is omitted.]

IV. ESTABLISH STRONG ORGANIZATIONS OF POOR AND LOWER-MIDDLE
PEASANTS

1) [See same numbered paragraph in Appendix C.]

2) Organizations of poor and lower-middle peasants, as pointed out by the Central Committee's draft resolution, should retain both their purity and their mass character. Participating in these organizations should be genuine poor and lower-middle peasants. In classifying the masses in the past, there were instances in which some upper-middle peasants, petty merchants, and even landlords and rich peasants were mistakenly classed as poor or lower-middle peasants. Also, some tenants or poor peasants were taken for middle peasants.

All these should be carefully corrected this time. We should strictly prevent false poor and lower-middle peasants from sneaking into the organizations of poor and lower-middle peasants; at the same time we should not bar genuine tenants or poor peasants from these organizations. Anyone who is seriously questionable in political or historical background, who has collaborated with the "four elements," and who has committed a serious mistake but has not repented after repeated warnings, should not be admitted to these organizations even if he is a poor or lower-middle peasant. Of the backbone elements in poor and lower-middle peasant organizations (for example, the chairmen of poor and lower-middle peasants' associations, committee members, and small group leaders), old tenants and poor peasants should constitute the absolute majority, while a certain number of lower-middle peasants should also be included. Also, a certain number of youths and women must be included in the backbone elements of poor and lower-middle peasant organizations. This provision will be helpful in strengthening the work with rural youths and women. When the poor and lower-middle peasant organizations begin to take shape, efforts should be made to recruit the great majority of poor and lower-middle peasants. In ethnically mixed regions, poor and lower-middle peasants of different ethnic groups should be recruited.

3) [See same numbered paragraph in Appendix C.]

4) [See same numbered paragraph in Appendix C. Paragraph 5 of Appendix C has been omitted.]

V. THE MIDDLE PEASANT PROBLEM

[The first two paragraphs duplicate the same two paragraphs of Appendix C, Section V. The third paragraph in Appendix C ("The upper-middle peasants . . .") is omitted. The 3rd, 4th, 5th, and 6th paragraphs then generally duplicate the 4th, 5th, 6th, and 7th paragraphs in Appendix C, except for the omission of the last sentence of the 6th paragraph.]

In view of the fact that some problems exist at present in the classification of various peasant classes, it is necessary for all comrades engaged in rural work to renew the study of the two documents concerning the classification of rural classes promulgated by the Central Committee in 1933, the supplementary resolutions by the Government Administrative Council of 1950, and several new resolutions of the Government Administrative Council, so as to better their understanding and make uniform the standard for class analysis.

The class backgrounds in rural villages, generally speaking, should be assessed on the basis of classifications carried out during the land reform and compared with the changes of status that took place before the collectivization. Since there is widespread confusion about class backgrounds in the villages it is necessary to clearly define class ranks as a part of the work of the Socialist Education Movement. The background of each rural household should be examined and classified after full discussions by the masses, and a class file be established. Any mistake in former classification should be duly corrected. In certain districts where the democratic revolution has not been thoroughly carried out, or in districts where no previous class classification has ever been made, a new classification program should be carried out.

The upper-middle peasant is a class with more serious tendency toward capitalism. In rural villages, one important aspect in the struggle between socialism and capitalism is the struggle between the lower-middle peasants' persistent work toward socialism and the upper-middle peasants' move toward capitalism. To deal with the upper-middle peasants' tendency toward capitalism, it is necessary to educate, criticize, and in some more serious cases, carry out necessary struggle measures. Otherwise, their wavering attitude cannot be corrected, their influence among the poor and lower-middle peasants cannot be checked, and the collective economy cannot be consolidated. Yet, they are laborers, and our friends. Any education, criticism or struggle measure is aimed at uniting them and holding them on the road of socialism, and enabling them to serve their proper function in production. Since the collectivization more than a decade ago, facts have proved that the great majority of upper-middle peasants are capable of following us on the road of socialism.

The conflict between us and the upper-middle peasants with a tendency toward capitalism is still an internal conflict of the people, and should be handled with care. When the poor and lower-middle peasants have been mobilized, this problem especially requires our attention. We should not oppose the upper-middle peasants as a whole. What we oppose are the ideology and activities of a few upper-middle peasants whose serious tendency toward capitalism runs counter to the interests of the state, the collective, and the commune members. However, in opposing a few upper-middle peasants for their tendency toward capitalism, we should not adopt the measures of struggle which we use against our enemy. We should not deprive them of their rights as commune members, brand them as capitalists, and, especially, encroach upon legal profits which they earn by joining in collective labor and laboring more than others. To push upper-middle peasants to the side of landlords and rich peasants will be most disadvantageous to us.

VI. UNIFY MORE THAN 95 PERCENT OF THE RURAL CADRES

During the initial stage of the Socialist Education Movement, Comrade Mao Tse-tung's directives of "persuasion and education, washing and bathing, going to the front with light burden, and consolidation against the enemy" were carried out in various places and over 95 percent of the cadres consolidated. The situation was encouraging. Our experience gained during the past year or so has proved that during the Socialist Education Movement, on the question of dealing with rural cadres, two deviations should be carefully prevented. When the masses have not yet been mobilized, the signs of Four Uncleans have not yet been exposed, and the struggle against capitalist and feudal influences has not yet been launched, we are apt to ignore the seriousness of problems among basic-level cadres and be not stern enough in the education and criticism of cadres who have committed mistakes. This is one of the deviations. When the lid on class struggle has completely been lifted and the masses have been fully mobilized, there may appear another deviation which includes failure to distinguish the conflict between the enemy and ourselves and the internal conflict of the people, exaggeration of the enemy's strength, and forming a bad opinion of basic-level cadres and even regarding them as the major target for our blows. Both deviations are harmful. Under the current circumstances, the former deviation is the major dangerous tendency which we should take care to prevent and correct. Before the masses are mobilized, we should stress the mobilization of the masses; after they are mobilized, we should stress practical handling of the problems. This is a question of experience in controlling the mass movement, and the art of leadership. Provincial, special district and hsien committees and all leading functionaries of work teams should master this art.

For the consolidation of over 95 percent of cadres, we must see clearly the following important questions and should adopt correct measures to solve them:

1) Our view on the vast number of basic-level cadres should be thoroughly

and not fragmentally analysed. Among basic-level rural cadres, many have committed big or small mistakes. They have not only committed the Four Uncleans economically, but also failed to draw the line between friend and enemy, lost their own stand, discriminated against poor and lower-middle peasants, hid their backgrounds and fabricated history, and so forth, thus committing the Four Uncleans politically and organizationally. The mistakes committed by some of them are more serious in nature. Some have even degenerated into agents and protectors of class enemies. Besides, a few landlords, rich peasants, counter-revolutionaries and undesirable elements have also infiltrated the revolutionary ranks. The problem, as we can see, is indeed serious. But on the other hand, we should also see that the great majority of basic-level rural cadres are good, or at least are basically good and can stand firm on the road of socialism under the Party's leadership. In the process of positive participation in the class and production struggle, their defects and mistakes can gradually be remedied and their ideological consciousness heightened. Among them, some 70 or 80 percent were tenant, poor or lower-middle peasants during the land reform period. The majority of them were also positive elements during the land reform and collectivization periods. What most of them have committed now are mostly limited to such common mistakes as excessive eating and unjustified possessions, petty theft, and having hazy class views. Only a small part of them have made serious mistakes. Of those basic-level cadres who have committed serious mistakes, the majority can reform provided that the masses are fully mobilized and that the Party deals with them correctly. Viewed in that light, over 95 percent of them can be consolidated.

2) What measures should be adopted to unify over 95 percent of the cadres? The only and correct way is to fully mobilize the masses, thoroughly expose contradictions, seriously carry out education, criticism or, if necessary, struggle, heighten the consciousness of the cadres, and enable them to "wash hands and take baths" and to correct their mistakes. As for cadres who have committed mistakes, with the exception of those degenerate elements who are beyond salvation, the work teams should at first entertain the hope of consolidating them. However, at the beginning and before the conclusion of the Four Cleans movement, consolidation can only be a hope. Only by firmly implementing the Central Committee's policies, fully mobilizing the masses, adopting correct methods, carefully carrying out the work, passing through criticism or struggle, and correctly solving existing contradictions, can we really consolidate over 95 percent of cadres on the basis of revolutionary principles. This is the method of "unity-criticism-unity" laid down by Comrade Mao Tse-tung—"to start from the hope for unity, to solve contradictions through criticism or struggle, and then to achieve new unity on a new basis."

During the Four Cleans movement, because of the fear of "hurting cadres' feelings," affecting the unity of the cadres, or of the cadres' quitting work, the work teams in some places assumed a tolerant attitude toward cadres who had committed even serious mistakes. They were afraid to criticize, to engage in struggle, and especially to mobilize the masses to solve their problems. They thought by these means they had achieved unity. Yet the result was that they were seriously divorced from the masses and achieved only a superficial, temporary and false consolidation of the cadres. This is a lesson that calls for our heightened vigilance.

To consolidate over 95 percent of rural cadres, we must first consolidate over 95 percent of the peasants. Only after over 95 percent of the peasants are consolidated can the consolidation of over 95 percent of cadres have a sound basis.

3) How to deal with basic-level organizations in the Socialist Education Movement? They should be treated differently according to the actual situation. When a basic-level organization can rely on the poor and lower-middle peasants, win their confidence, stand firm on the socialist road or is good basically, the working team should rely on it for carrying out its work programs. But this should be after the masses have been fully mobilized and the organization proved to be such a basic-level organization. As for those basic-level organizations which are divorced from the poor and lower-middle peasants, or have damaged the interests of such peasants, and those with more serious problems, only after the Four Cleans movement has been carried out, their problems truly solved and the confidence of poor and lower-middle peasants won, can they be relied upon to carry out the work. Basic-level organizations in which the leadership has been taken over by landlords, rich peasants, counter-revolutionaries and undesirable elements or is controlled by degenerate elements should be reorganized. But the reorganization should not be carried out until the poor and lower-middle peasant masses are mobilized and organized and the situation is confirmed by investigations. Of course, we should consolidate those good Party members and cadres among them and work with them.

On the question of relying on the poor and lower-middle peasants and the basic-level organizations, our policy is: reliance on the poor and lower-middle peasants is the basic and decisive factor of the whole program. We rely on basic-level organizations because they represent the interests of poor and lower-middle peasants. Therefore, the purpose of relying on basic-level organizations is reliance upon poor and lower-middle peasants.

4) [See subsection 2 of Appendix C, Section VI.]

(a) [See subsection 2(a) of Appendix C, Section VI. However, the following addition is made to the first sentence: "Concerning cadres who have committed mistakes, *we must let them make self-examinations before the masses and receive the criticism of the masses; at the same time* we should assume the attitude . . ."]

(b) [See subsection 2(b) of Appendix C, Section VI.]

(c) Do a good job in financial reimbursement and compensation. Money and valuables obtained through corruption or theft, regardless of amounts, must be reimbursed or compensated in full. As for those who engage in speculation, profiteering or making high-interest loans (including such persons in the society or among the peasants), they should in accordance with the law and our policies, be ordered to pay up their taxes or to return the interest collected, or be fined, or their illegal gains confiscated. In short, those who have committed such mistakes should not be allowed to make financial gains, so that they learn a lesson and not repeat such mistakes. However, the calculation should be practical and the reimbursement, retrospective tax payment, and fines should be reasonable. These must be both satisfactory to the masses and acceptable to the wrongdoers. The period for calculating the reimbursement and compensation should not be too long. Except for gang leaders of corrupting, stealing, speculating, profiteering groups or repeated offenders, the period for calculating the reimbursement and compensation may begin from the time when the first revised draft of the 60 Articles was passed down to the villages, that is, the latter half of 1961. If the valuables gained through corruption and theft are still retrievable, they should be retrieved; if not, they may be paid for at fixed prices. As for what should be the prices of the valuables, it should be discussed and duly decided upon within the brigade. If the offender cannot afford to pay for it all at once, he may pay by installments.

If those who have committed corruption, theft, speculation or profiteering have confessed and made reimbursement or compensation, they can be excused from the charges if the indignation of the people is not too serious. However they should no longer be permitted to continue to be cadres or in charge of money or valuables. If the offenders' attitude is bad, the cases serious, or the people's indignation great, then they should, upon approval by the hsien people's council, be charged with corruption, stealing, speculating or profiteering, and be sentenced to labor under the supervision of the masses. The speculating and profiteering elements in society and among the peasants can also be handled in accordance with these principles.

The cadres' mistakes of excessive eating and unjustified possession should all be severely criticized. In cases of large-scale excessive eating and unjustified possession, reimbursement and compensation should be effected. If the offender cannot afford to reimburse or compensate for all at once, he may do so by installments. If he has done a good job in self-review and criticism, the amount of reimbursement or compensation may be duly reduced, upon agreement of the masses. In cases of ordinary excessive eating or unjustified possession, if the amounts involved are small and if the self-criticism is satisfactory and the masses agree, the offender may be excused from making reimbursement or compensation. Yet, at places where the Four Cleans movement has already been carried out, or where the Central Committee's draft resolutions or the draft of these policy decisions have already been announced, any offense of excessive eating or unjustified possession, regardless of the amount involved, should be reimbursed or compensated for in full. The period set for the calculation of this offense should begin from 1962.

(d) Do a good job in handling by the organization. An offender who confesses on his own accord, and does a satisfactory job in self-criticism, reimbursement and compensation, may be handled with leniency or excused. In cases of serious offense, or unsatisfactory confession, reimbursement or compensation, or if the masses consider punishment necessary, then diciplinary action should be taken. The punishment should be appropriate. The offender should be given whatever punishment he deserves. The scope of punishment should be strictly controlled. Except for degenerate elements who are beyond salvation, or former landlords, rich peasants, counter-revolutionaries, and undesirable elements who have sneaked into the cadres' ranks (such persons should be purged completely), it is probably proper that the total number of cadres receiving such punishment as expulsion from the Party membership or dismissal from their administrative positions be fixed at around one percent and below two percent, with the hsien as a unit. In every province, there are several hsien with special circumstances. The percentages of punishment-receiving cadres in different hsien should be fixed by provincial, municipal and autonomous region Party committees on the basis of actual circumstances.

Wrong-doing cadres should be handled with caution, seriousness and practicality. Data exposed during the Movement should be double-checked and confirmed and 100 percent sure. Cadres should be dealt with after careful analyses and studies are made and the nature of the problem and seriousness of the case become very clear.

Cadres who have committed mistakes should be allowed to defend themselves on questions exposed by others or confessed by themselves. Any problem in which it cannot be readily decided whether it is a contradiction between enemy and ourselves or an internal contradiction of the people, should first be handled as an internal contradiction of the people. Except for individual cases or cases that cannot wait, generally all cases should be handled at the latter stage of the movement, when the leadership and the masses have comparatively cooled down. Yet they should all be handled and concluded before the work team leaves the village. Matters requiring approval of higher levels should also be approved by the higher-level organization before the work team leaves the village. Questions which cannot be cleared for the time being should be listed as special cases to be examined and handled by a committee left behind by the work team.

After the Socialist Education Movement, if a cadre who has committed a mistake and received punishment, should commit such serious acts of anti-Party, anti-people or anti-socialism as plotting for a counter-offensive, retaliation by returning blows, and obstruction of the collective economy, he must be branded as a counter-revolutionary and dealt with accordingly. He must be expelled from the Party if a member.

5) Experience gained in the Socialist Education Movement at various places during the past year or so has revealed that cadres in basic-level organizations who have committed serious mistakes are usually connected with certain cadres of higher-level organizations or other organizations, and are instigated, supported and protected by them. In such cases, we must go to the origin and get hold of the responsible persons. No matter to what level the cadres belong, or what positions they hold, as long as they have collaborated with undesirable cadres of basic-level organizations and done bad things, they should be subjected to open criticisms before the people in the place concerned. In more serious cases, proper punishments should be meted out.

6) [See subsection 3 in Appendix C, Section VI.]

VII. CONCERNING CADRE PARTICIPATION IN COLLECTIVE PRODUCTION LABOR

[The first three paragraphs duplicate the same paragraphs in Appendix C. To the 4th paragraph in Appendix C, the following has been added:] We must make every cadre understand that many mistakes found among cadres are all connected with their failure to participate in collective labor. The divorce from collective labor is the beginning of degeneration.

[The 5th paragraph duplicates the same paragraph of Appendix C. In the 6th paragraph, the following sentence has been inserted between the two sentences of this paragraph in Appendix C.] No unauthorized subsidy of work points under any excuse is allowed.

[The remainder of Section VII is as in Appendix C.]

VIII. SCRUPULOUS READJUSTMENT OF BASIC PARTY ORGANIZATIONS IN RURAL VILLAGES

[The first two paragraphs generally duplicate the same two paragraphs of Appendix C.]

Party reform in the villages is being carried out in close coordination with other programs of the Socialist Education Movement. The whole process of the Socialist Education Movement is the reform of the Party's basic-level organizations. The Party rectification calls for the following steps:

1) All Party members must take an intensive course in class and socialist education, a course in the basic knowledge of the Party and the standard of a Party member, so that every member will be able to distinguish between friend and foe, between socialist and capitalistic roads, between the vanguard group and the masses.

2) Thoroughly expose and seriously solve problems within Party organizations. Carry out a full examination and rating of Party members' social class origins, class standpoint, political history, thought and work style, and work performance.

3) [See same numbered paragraph in Appendix C.]

4) Party members who have committed serious or comparatively serious mistakes and failed to repent after repeated persuasions, who are constantly pessimistic and backward and who show no improvement after repeated educational sessions, and who are below the Party member's standards, should be separately and properly dealt with by the organization.

5) [See same numbered paragraph in Appendix C.]

6) [See same numbered paragraph in Appendix C.]

7) [See same numbered paragraph in Appendix C.]

8) From the beginning of the Movement, attention should be directed to developing activist elements with good background, firm stand and persistence in their work for socialism, for admission into the Party in the latter part of the Movement after both the Party and the poor and lower-middle peasant masses have discussed and agreed on their qualifications.

When the eight steps mentioned above are carried out, the Party's basic organizations in the villages can be said to have been fundamentally rectified, and the registration of Party members completed.

[The last paragraph duplicates the penultimate paragraph in Appendix C, Section VIII, down to ". . . approval by higher authorities." The remainder of the penultimate paragraph and the final paragraph in this Section of Appendix C are omitted.]

IX. Handling of Landlords, Rich Peasants, Counter-revolutionaries, and Undesirable Elements

During the Socialist Education Movement, *we must assign a special stage to mobilize the masses and develop struggle with the enemy; moreover* we must correctly handle the problems of landlords, rich peasants, counter-revolutionaries and various types of bad elements. [Emphasis indicates added material. Remainder of paragraph duplicates Appendix C.]

[In the middle of the second paragraph of Appendix C—following ". . . under 5 percent)"—there is inserted the sentence:] The method of reforming them on the spot by relying upon the strength of the masses should be adopted.

[The text then duplicates the 3rd, 4th, 5th, and 6th paragraphs in Appendix C—through the paragraph ending ". . . dictatorial treatment should be carried out."]

Both in the south and in the north, there are places where the democratic revolution has not been, or is far from being, thoroughly carried out. In this movement, remedial study of democratic revolution must be seriously pushed. In those places, only when the democratic revolution has been thoroughly carried out can the Socialist Education Movement proceed smoothly.

Landlords and rich peasants who were left out of the black list during the land reform should now be picked out; any of them engaged in sabotaging activities should be branded "landlord" or "rich peasant," upon approval of the hsien people's council. Any of them who has shown good or fair performance may be freed from the labels of "landlord" or "rich peasant," after discussion and approval by the poor and lower-middle peasant organization, but their original backgrounds should be announced to the masses.

[The final paragraph duplicates the same paragraph in Appendix C except for the omission of the final sentence of the Appendix C text.]

X. Correct Handling of the Question of How to Deal with Sons and Daughters of Landlords and Rich Peasants

[The first sentence of the first paragraph of the Appendix C text is omitted; otherwise the first five paragraphs in Appendix C are duplicated.]

Children of landlords and rich peasants should be barred without exception from taking the positions of local basic-level leading cadres. Generally they are also unfit for such important positions as accountants, custodians, cashiers, enterprise and business administrative functionaries of communes or production brigades. Yet, some young students, employees or workers returning to work in their native villages, and rehabilitated soldiers from landlord and rich peasant families, after a longer time of satisfactory examination, may be given suitable work assignments (including social work), on the basis of actual needs. They should also be educated and remolded during the work.

Education of Party members, Young Communist League members, basic-level cadres, poor and lower-middle peasants married to children of landlords and rich peasants should be strengthened, to teach them to heighten vigilance, to guard against falling into traps of the class enemy, to draw a clear political line, to be firm on class stand, and not to be affected by the enemy's bad influences. Whether or not Party members, Young Communist League members, and cadres married to sons and daughters of landlords and rich peasants can become cadres should mainly depend upon their personal performance, not simply upon the fact that they are married to children of landlords and rich peasants. If these people are seriously affected by the enemy's bad influences, then they should be handled with strictness. In especially serious cases, they should be deprived of their Party membership, citizenship, or their cadre positions.

[The final paragraph duplicates the final paragraph in Appendix C.]

APPENDIX F (THE TWENTY-THREE ARTICLES)*

CHINESE COMMUNIST PARTY
CENTRAL COMMITTEE DOCUMENT NO. (65) 026
Printed by the Fukien Provincial Party Committee
General Office, January, 18, 1965. *Fu* No. 001

(Confidential)

SOME PROBLEMS CURRENTLY ARISING IN THE COURSE OF THE RURAL SOCIALIST EDUCATION MOVEMENT†

NOTICE: To regional bureaus of the Central Committee; province, municipality, and autonomous region Party committees; Party member groups of the various central ministries and commissions; and the General Political Department of the Military Affairs Committee.

The Politburo of the Central Committee convened a National Work Conference, discussed some problems currently arising in the course of the rural Socialist Education Movement, and wrote a summary of the discussions. We now send you this document. If this document should contradict previous Central Committee documents concerning the Socialist Education Movement then this document shall uniformly be taken as the standard.

This document should be issued to Party committees at and above the hsien and regiment levels, and to the Party committees of work brigades and teams.

The Central Committee, January 14, 1965

A SUMMARY OF THE DISCUSSIONS OF THE NATIONAL WORK CONFERENCE CONVENED BY THE POLITBURO OF THE CENTRAL COMMITTEE, JANUARY 14, 1965

I. *The Situation*

Since the tenth plenum of the eighth Central Committee in September 1962, through the development of socialist education in urban areas as well as the countryside, the execution of a series of Central Committee policies by the whole Party, the active efforts of the masses, the broad number of Party members, and cadres, a very good situation has come into being on the political, economic, ideological and cultural, and military fronts in our country. In the past few months, in the entire country more than one million cadres went deeply into the basic level units in the cities and countryside, and the socialist revolutionary movement manifested a new high tide.

All the great accomplishments which our country obtained so quickly during the past few years prove the Party's general line of building socialism is correct, and at the same time prove further that the Chinese Communist

---

* Translated from a photocopy of a Chinese typescript original supplied to the authors by officials of the Institute of International Relations, Republic of China. The copy of the Chinese original is located in the Center for Chinese Studies Library, University of California, Berkeley. The present translation has been further checked against a Japanese translation, published as: Chukyo Chuo Seiji-kyoku (Political Bureau, CCP Central Committee), "Shakai-shugi kyoiku undo no ni-ju-san kajo" (The Twenty-three Points of the Socialist Education Movement), *Sekai* (The World), No. 256 (March, 1967), pp. 121–29.

† *Nung-ts'un she-hui chu-i chiao-yü yün-tung chung mu-ch'ien t'i-ch'u ti i-hsieh wen-t'i*

Party led by Comrade Mao Tse-tung is a glorious, great and correct party. Our Party will not betray the trust and hopes of the people of the whole nation and of the people of the world.

In our cities and villages alike, there exists serious, acute class struggle. After the socialist reform of the ownership system was basically completed, the class enemies who oppose socialism attempted to use the form of "peaceful evolution" to restore capitalism. This situation of class struggle is necessarily reflected within the Party. The leadership of certain communes, brigades, enterprises and units has either been corrupted or usurped.

In our work, in the process of moving forward, there exist a great many problems. Practice proves that as long as the whole Party penetratingly and correctly continues to execute the Central Committee's various decisions concerning the Socialist Education Movement, continues to grasp the principles of class struggle, continues to rely on the working class, the poor and lower-middle peasants, the revolutionary cadres, the revolutionary intellectuals and other revolutionary elements, and continues to pay close attention to uniting more than 95 percent of our people and 95 percent of our cadres, then the many problems which exist in the cities and in the villages will not only be easy to discover, but will also be easy to resolve.

We must resolutely continue the Socialist Education Movement of the past two years and more, and carry it through to the end; we absolutely must not falter.

The present problem is to sum up the past experience of this movement, assess our achievements, and overcome the shortcomings in our work in order to facilitate an even greater victory.

II. *The Nature of the Movement*

Several ways of presentation:

1) The contradiction between the Four Cleans and the Four Uncleans;

2) The overlapping of contradictions within the Party and contradictions outside of the Party, or the overlapping of contradictions between the enemy and us and contradictions within the people;

3) The contradiction between socialism and capitalism.

The former two ways do not clarify the fundamental characteristics of the Socialist Education Movement. These two approaches do not refer to what society the contradiction of the Four Cleans and Four Uncleans arises in. Nor do they indicate what the nature is of the overlapping of contradictions within the Party and contradictions outside of the Party. They also do not indicate in what historical period the overlapping of contradictions between the enemy and us and contradictions within the people arises nor the class content of this overlapping. If we take a literal point of view, the so-called Four Cleans and Four Uncleans could be applied to any society in past history and the so-called overlapping of contradictions within the Party and contradictions outside the Party could be applied to any party. The so-called overlapping of contradictions between the enemy and us and contradictions within the people could be applied to any historical period. These approaches do not explain the nature of today's contradictions; therefore they are not Marxist-Leninist methods of looking at things.

The last way of presenting the nature of the movement comprehends the essence of the question, and is Marxist-Leninist. It is decidedly in accord with the scientific theories of Comrade Mao Tse-tung, and with the policies adopted by the Central Committee at various times since the second plenum of the Seventh Central Committee in 1949, concerning the continued existence, during the entire transitional period, of class contradictions, class struggle between the proletariat and the bourgeoisie, and struggle between the two roads of socialism and capitalism.

If we forget the basic theory and basic practice of our Party during the past decade and a half, we will go astray.

The key point of this movement is to rectify those people in positions of authority within the Party who take the capitalist road, and to progressively consolidate and develop the socialist battlefront in the urban and rural areas.

Of those people in positions of authority who take the capitalist road, some are out in the open and some are concealed. Of the people who support them, some are at lower levels and some are at higher levels. Among those lower down, some have already been classified as landlords, rich peasants, counter-revolutionaries and bad elements, while others have been overlooked.

Among those at higher levels, there are some people in the communes, districts, hsien, special districts, and even in the work of provincial and Central Committee departments, who oppose socialism. Among them some were originally alien class elements; some are degenerate elements who have shed their original skin and changed their nature; and some have received bribes, banded together for seditious purposes, violated the law, and violated discipline.

Certain people do not distinguish the boundary between the enemy and ourselves; they have lost their class standpoint; and they harbor, within their own families and among their own friends and fellow workers, those people who engage in capitalist activities.

The great majority of our cadres want to take the socialist road, but there are some among them who have but a hazy knowledge of the socialist revolution, who employ personnel improperly, who are haphazard about checking up on work, and who commit the mistake of bureaucratism.

III. *A Unified Way of Presentation*

The Socialist Education Movement in the cities and countryside will from now on be uniformly simplified as the Four Cleans Movement—clean politics, clean economics, clean organization, and clean ideology.

In the past, the Socialist Education Movement in the cities was called the "Five Anti" movement. From now on we will call it the Four Cleans Movement and will abolish the "Five Anti."

IV. *Setting Good Standards for the Movement*

At the June 1964 meeting of the Standing Committee of the Politburo of the Central Committee attended by the first secretaries of the regional bureaus of the Central Committee, Comrade Mao Tse-tung said:

> What are good standards for evaluation of the Socialist Education Movement?
>
> 1) We must see whether the poor and lower-middle peasants have been truly aroused.
>
> 2) Has the problem of the Four Uncleans among the cadres been resolved?
>
> 3) Have the cadres participated in physical labor?
>
> 4) Has a good leadership nucleus been established?
>
> 5) When landlords, rich peasants, counter-revolutionaries and bad elements who engage in destructive activities are discovered, is this contradiction merely turned over to the higher levels, or are the masses mobilized to strictly supervise, criticize, and even appropriately struggle against these elements, and moreover retain them for reform on the spot?
>
> 6) We must see whether production is increasing or decreasing.

At that time, the Standing Committee of the Politburo held that these standards for assessing whether the Socialist Education Movement was being carried out properly were fully appropriate.

V. *Work Methods*

1) Within the movement as a whole, provincial, special district, and hsien level party committees and work teams, relying on the great majority of the masses and cadres (including cadres who have cast aside their misgivings and doubts), must gradually carry out the "3 unifications" with respect to the masses, cadres, and work teams.

2) Once the movement has begun, we must immediately explain its meaning to the cadres and masses, and we must inform them of our policies. We must clearly declare that, no matter what commune or brigade, and no matter whether during or after the movement, the use of pretexts for opposing the masses of commune members will not be permitted.

3) The work teams must, during the movement and during the process of struggle, arouse the poor and lower-middle peasants, organize class ranks, discover activist elements and train them to form a leadership nucleus, and work together with them. We must not be quiet; we must not be mysterious; and we must not confine our activities to a small minority of the people.

4) In the course of the movement, from start to finish we must grasp production. At the same time, we must pay attention to grasping each year's distribution (the question of livelihood). If we do not grasp the questions of production and distribution, we will become divorced from the masses and will bring grievous harm to our cause.

5) We must proceed on the basis of local conditions. Reality demands this. Whatever problems the masses require to be solved must be solved. Whatever imbalances occur in our work must be rectified.

6) In the movement, we must boldly unleash the masses; we must not be like women with bound feet—we must not bind our hands and feet. At the same time, we must make a deep and fine penetration, and must not make a big fuss over nothing. We must set the facts in order, explain principles, eliminate simple, crude work methods, severely prohibit beating people and other forms of physical punishment, and prevent forced confessions.

7) To sum up: in the course of the movement as a whole, we must make use of contradictions to win over the majority, oppose the minority, and attack and defeat all who persist in taking the capitalist road—always a very small minority. Some people have committed mistakes which can still be rectified. With regard to those people who are the target of the Four Cleans movement, we must be good at discriminating among them and treating them differentially, taking the worst people and isolating them or narrowly confining them.

VI. *Concentrate Our Forces, Fight a War of Annihilation*

In leading the movement, we must have an overall, balanced point of view and an overall, balanced deployment. We must, through preliminary investigation and study, carry out a preliminary ordering of our ranks. We must suitably concentrate our forces to fight a war of annihilation. Starting in those key areas where the greatest number of problems exist, and where the influence [of those problems] is great, we must first make a breakthrough at a [single] point and then have an all-around thrust.

Point work does not refer merely to our working within production brigades, for we must also appropriately unite upper and lower level bodies as well as different bodies at the same level.

The movement should develop group by group and phase by phase like the motion of a wave—first resolving problems at one place and then moving on to resolve problems elsewhere.

The various provinces and cities should have the right to allocate their forces, and when necessary they may concentrate their cadres for training purposes during the course of the movement.

We should not rely on human sea tactics. We must not concentrate excessively large work teams within a single hsien, commune, or brigade. In this way, more points can be dealt with at the same time. This will also help us to follow the mass line.

The main thing is to go all out to prepare a nucleus of cadres who are able to grasp the Party's policy and who are able to understand and follow the mass line.

VII. *Squatting at Points*

"If one has not investigated, then one has no right of expression."

This teaching of Comrade Mao Tse-tung must be observed in our work. The effective investigation and research methods used by our Party in the past, such as that of holding investigation meetings, should continue to be utilized. Squatting at a point and dissecting a sparrow [i.e. making a thorough and careful analysis—transl.] is a very important method of leadership. Leading cadres must in a selective and planned manner continue to squat at points, going down to the basic levels and penetrating into the masses and, in the course of the movement and struggle, gaining relatively systematic experience.

There can be different methods of squatting at points. There should be a group of people who, for a relatively long period of time, go down into a brigade to guide the movement to its completion from beginning to end.

The leading personnel of Party organizations at the Central Committee regional bureau, provincial, special district, and hsien levels must implement the leadership methods which combine the general and individual aspects. Besides selecting a locality for squatting, they can convene meetings in places where they are squatting themselves or in other places, and carry out investigation, research and guidance of work in other points, and of production and other kinds of work in whole regions, provinces, special districts and hsien on the plane.

They can also go on inspection tours of other places, or organize small-scale roving inspection groups in order to facilitate their grasping of an active attitude, the mutual communication of information, and the exchange of experience.

VIII. *Grasping Work on the Plane*

We must look after both points and the plane.

At present the plane, outside of the key points which are carrying out the Four Cleans movement, constitutes the great majority of the country. The main task in these areas is production and construction. This task must conscientiously be well done.

The Central Committee bureaus, provincial committees, and special district committees must grasp the work of entire regions, provinces, and special districts.

With regard to work on the plane, these committees must also appropriately carry on the work of socialist education, of raising the political consciousness of the cadres, and of stimulating the latter to self-awaredly cleanse their hands and bodies. We should clearly declare to them that if their problems are not great, or if their problems are many but they confess and make restitution, and as long as they perform their work and make up for their errors with achievements, then we will not go into these things that are past.

Some hsien on the plane, if they have the proper conditions and the approval of the provincial committee, can also carry out Four Cleans point testing work.

The training of cadres in some localities can be used as reference for effective methods in developing from point to plane.

IX. *The Cadre Question*

1) In dealing with the cadre question, we must use the method of "one divides into two." We should adopt a serious, positive, and affectionate attitude toward them.

2) The situation will gradually become clarified. There are four possible types of cadres: good, relatively good, those with many problems, and those whose mistakes are of a serious nature. Under general conditions, cadres of the first two types are in the majority.

3) Comrade Mao Tse-tung long ago said: "We must adopt the policy of 'warn a man first so he may afterwards exert himself to goodness' and 'treating the illness to save the man' in dealing with people who make mistakes." He also said, "We must make a distinction between those party members and cadres who have committed mistakes, but who can still be educated, and those who cannot be saved. No matter what their backgrounds, we must step up their education and must not discard them." At the present time, we must continue to heed these instructions of Comrade Mao Tse-tung.

The policy we ought to adopt toward those cadres who have committed mistakes is "to persuade them to accept education, cleanse their hands and bodies, go to battle unencumbered, and unite against the enemy." It is a policy which arises from a profound hope for unity; one which, through criticism or struggle, brings about the resolution of contradictions; and which then attains a new unity on a new foundation.

4) Toward those cadres who have committed minor Four Unclean mistakes or who, though they have had many problems, have freely confessed their past histories, we ought to do our utmost to quickly liberate them. Toward those cadres whose mistakes are of a nature which is presently unclear, and who may therefore have been unsuitably retained at their original work posts, we may change their work or give them concentrated training, and carry on investigation of their cases.

5) Economic indemnities must not be randomly or unsystematically imposed. At the same time, such indemnities must accord with the actual conditions and with reason. In cases where the problems are not serious, and where examination and criticism has been relatively good, if the masses so agree, such indemnities may be reduced, delayed, or even cancelled.

6) We must adopt necessary and suitable disciplinary measures toward those cadres who have committed mistakes. This is for the purpose of educating and transforming them. As long as they are willing to take the socialist road, the Party will unite with them, and the masses will unite with them.

Of those incompetent cadres, some can be regulated and some can be transformed. Those Party members who do not fulfill the conditions of membership can be exhorted to leave the Party. These cases can all be dealt with in the latter stage of the movement.

7) Where the nature of the mistakes is serious—where leadership authority has been taken over by alien class elements or by degenerate elements who have shed their skin and changed their nature—authority must be seized, first by struggle and then by removing these elements from their positions. In general, the question of their membership in the Party should be resolved later. In cases which are especially serious, these elements can be fired from

their posts on the spot, their Party membership cards taken away, and they may even, if need be, be forcibly detained. Counter-revolutionaries, landlords, rich peasants and bad elements who have wormed their way into the Party must all be expelled from the Party.

In places where authority must be seized, or under conditions where the peoples' militia organization is critically impure, we should adopt the method of turning over the weapons and ammunition of the peoples' militia to reliable elements among the poor and lower-middle peasants.

8) When necessary, individual counter-revolutionaries or bad elements who have severely coerced the masses may be placed temporarily under guard or sent to do physical labor in the countryside until their cases are judged. In the most serious cases, such as murder, arson, or other serious crimes where the culprit is actually caught in the act, they may be arrested and their cases dealt with by legal channels.

9) Some bad cadres may have formed cliques. We must guard against classifying too many groups as cliques, or classifying the membership of the cliques too broadly.

X. *Establishing Poor and Lower-Middle Peasants' Associations*

Poor and Lower-Middle Peasants' Associations are revolutionary class organizations of a mass nature voluntarily organized by the poor and lower-middle peasants under the leadership of the Communist Party. These organizations supervise and assist cadres of various levels within the people's communes in carrying out work. This type of organization will fully develop its functions in the consolidation of the dictatorship of the proletariat, the consolidation of the collective economy, and the development of collective production.

The poor and lower-middle peasants, and their labor power in production, make up 60 to 70 percent of the total population and labor power in the countryside. They constitute the great majority. Poor peasants' associations, once they have been organized, may attract prosperous middle peasants and other people who have ambitions of self-advancement. These latter elements will try to ally with those people whose attitude toward socialism is normally wavering.

During the course of the Socialist Education Movement, in those places where basic-level organizations have atrophied or become paralyzed, and before a new leadership nucleus has been formed, we may implement [the policy of] all power to the poor and lower-middle peasants' associations.

XI. *The Question of Time*

For a brigade, about half a year; for a hsien, a year or more. Estimating from the fall and winter of 1964, about three years will be needed to complete the movement throughout one-third of our country. Within six or seven years, the movement will be completed throughout the whole country. So long as our policies and work methods are correct, the pace of the movement may be accelerated somewhat.

XII. *Declaration of Policies Concerning Concealed Lands*

After free and open discussion by the masses, the state will refrain for a period of about five years from increasing burdens on, and will not make further procurements from, those lands which have been concealed.

XIII. *The Work of Finance and Trade Departments Must be Adjusted to Fit the Four Cleans Movement*

Increasing burdens or the repayment of loans will not be permitted simply because a certain place has already carried out the Four Cleans movement. Finance and trade organs, with respect to investment and loans, ought suitably to support production and construction in those areas which are carrying out the Four Cleans movement.

XIV. *The Composition of Work Teams*

It is not necessary to be fully and completely "clean." Those who have committed mistakes may also participate, on the one hand to facilitate their education and transformation, and on the other hand so that some of them can gain an all-around view of the movement and thus become useful workers. The work teams must continually summarize experiences and fix times for readjustment.

XV. *Providing a Way Out*

With regard to landlords, rich peasants, counter-revolutionaries, bad elements, and elements who have shed their skin and changed their nature, under the supervision of the masses they must undergo reform through labor in order to help them turn over a new leaf. Among those persons who have committed serious Four Unclean mistakes, some are no longer cadres or party members. These persons may still, however, be allowed to serve as commune members, to work diligently. Of the landlords, rich peasants, counter-revolutionaries and other bad elements who have labored honestly and have not done bad deeds for the past decade or more, there are some who have already been labelled. Can these labels be removed? Others have not yet been labelled; can they be excused from again being labelled? These questions should be judged and decided by the masses.

XVI. *The Four Cleans Movement Must Rest Firmly on Construction*

Speaking of a single hsien, both during and after the Four Cleans movement the work of training a party leadership nucleus must be gradually done. All instruments of the proletarian dictatorship must gradually be grasped in the hands of reliable people. A socialist hsien must gradually be solidly built up in order to enable the work of production, construction, science, culture, education, health and sanitation, public safety and the peoples' militia to make progress.

Production and construction in each commune and brigade throughout the country will be like a great fortress through upholding the policy of relying on one's own efforts.

XVII. *The Size of Production Teams*

During the process of the Four Cleans movement, after thorough discussion by the poor and lower-middle peasants, and after having been decided by the masses, production teams may carry out adjustment or organizational reform. Is a figure of about thirty households per team reasonable? If people live in relatively tight concentrations, the figure of thirty households may be exceeded. If people are relatively widely dispersed, less than thirty may be appropriate. These matters should not be decided from above.

XVIII. *The Tenure of Office of Basic-Level Cadres*

In accordance with the "60 articles," we should set a time to carry out democratic elections. Terms of office for reelection, or reappointment should in general be limited to four years. Cadres who are corrupt, who have committed serious mistakes, or who are unable to perform their duties well, may be recalled at any time.

XIX. *The Question of Supervision*

Cadres must be supervised both from above and from below. The most important supervision is that which comes from the masses. During the Four Cleans movement, cadres and masses should explore effective supervisory and political work systems. The authority of supervisory organs must be greater than that of the administrative organs of the same level.

XX. *Four Great Democracies*

All communes and brigades must learn from the People's Liberation Army and carry out political democracy, democracy in production, democracy in financial affairs, and military democracy.

XXI. *Work Attitudes*

All talk—good, bad, correct, and incorrect—must be listened to. It is particularly dissent that we must patiently listen to. We must let people fully express themselves.

XXII. *Methods of Thought*

We must strive to avoid one-sidedness and partialness. Everything must be analyzed, no matter what it is.

To view everything as absolute, motionless, isolated and unchanging is metaphysical. To spend one's time cataloguing great piles of superficial phenomena, or compiling great quantities of rules and regulations is scholasticism, which renders people unable to receive the necessary leadership. We must be proponents of dialectical materialism; we must oppose metaphysics and scholasticism.

XXIII. *Scope*

The various points raised above should, in principle, be applied also to the Four Cleans movement in the cities.

GLOSSARY

17	lao-tung	勞動	labor
17	kung-tso	工作	work
18	pu-t'ieh kung-fen	補貼工分	subsidized work-points
18	san ting	三定	"three fixes"
20	shih tien	試點	"spot testing"
21	ling-tao ho-hsin	領導核心	leadership nucleus
23	tun tien	蹲點	"squatting at points"
25	i wan ch'ün-chung	億萬群眾	countless masses
25	chieh-chi tou-cheng i chua chiu ling	階級鬥爭， 一抓就靈	once class struggle is grasped, miracles are possible
32	chien-tu	監督	supervise, supervision
35	ch'ing-li	清理	"cleaning-up"
35	chi-pen chien-she	基本建設	basic construction
36	chiao ch'a	交叉	overlapping
37	cheng	整	rectify
38	san chieh-ho	三結合	three-way alliances
43	tzu-li keng-sheng	自力更生	self-reliance
43	tzu-wo hsi-sheng	自我犧牲	self-sacrifice

128